BUSINESS VALUATION BLUEBOOK

How Successful Entrepreneurs Price, Buy, Sell and Trade Businesses

Chad Simmons
Facts On Demand Press

Business Valuation Bluebook
How Successful Entrepreneurs Price, Buy, Sell and Trade Businesses

Edited by Nancy Crisp. Cover Design by Rocks-Dehart Public Relations. Interior Design by Steve Sneed, Marble Tree. Printed in the United States by Mennonite Press.

Copyright © 2002 by Chad Simmons
Simmons Investment Company, LLC
4200 Somerset, Suite 245
Prairie Village, KS 66208
Voice 888-649-7785   Fax 913-385-7747
Website: www.ceband.com

Facts on Demand Press
PO Box 27869
Tempe, AZ 85285-7869
Voice 800-929-3811 Fax 800-929-3810
Website www.brbpub.com

Publisher's Cataloging-in-Publication Data

Simmons, Chad
    Business Valuation Bluebook: how successful
    Entrepreneurs price, sell and trade businesses / Chad Simmons. – 2nd ed.

    p. cm.
    Includes index.
    ISBN: 1-899150-32-0

    1. Business enterprises—Valuation—Handbooks,
    manuals, etc. 2. Sale of business enterprises—
    Handbooks, manuals, etc. 3. Business enterprises—
    Purchasing—Handbooks, manuals, etc.   I.Title.

    HD1393.25.S56 2002   658.1'6
                  QBI02-200028

About the Author

Chad Simmons is an expert on small business valuation. He teaches what he does and does what he teaches – a symbol of today's entrepreneur.

Chad gained national standing in his franchise company selling small businesses. He rose through the ranks to become the company's president and a principal stockholder. His company was America's largest country real estate franchiser. In addition to rural property sales the company sold $40 to $50 Million of small businesses and commercial properties each year. Afterward, he wrote the Business Valuation Bluebook describing his small business valuation techniques.

Nearly 50 colleges have acquired his materials for classroom use. Chad's books and seminars have been included in the prestigious CCIM continuing education program sponsored by the National Association of Realtors. He has taught small business valuation, approved for continuing education credit in several states, for nearly 20 years nationwide.

His most recent venture is the launch of CEband, an Internet company that provides professional seminars online including Small Business Valuation. His Internet delivery system is certified by two prestigious organizations: the Association of Real Estate License Law Officials (ARELLO) and the International Distance Education Certification Center (IDECC). His Small Business Valuation online seminar has been used as continuing education credit for real estate, appraisal and insurance and related business professionals. This and other courses may be viewed at www.ceband.com. He is also an active real estate investor. Chad's hobbies include amateur astronomy, woodworking, reading and spending time with his family in Leawood, Kansas. He enjoys visualizing and executing ideas to improve business results.

Other Books & Works by Chad Simmons:

The Anonymous Entrepreneur
Small Business Valuation Online

Look Who's Talking About The First Edition of the
BUSINESS VALUATION BLUEBOOK

Finalist
ForeWord Magazine's 2000 Business Book of the Year

FORTUNE SMALL BUSINESS - *"Chad Simmons says, 'The point is to sell before your company hits the peak, but not when valuations in your industry are too low.'"*

BIZLIFE - *"The Business Valuation Bluebook will give you the edge to sell for the highest possible price and buy at the lowest."*

JOHN HUGHES, CHAIRMAN, THE COLEMAN FOUNDATION - *"A timely publication that will be a time saver to entrepreneurs as they grow their businesses through acquisitions or 'cash-out' businesses they have created."*

WHAT'S WORKING IN CONSULTING - *"The Business Valuation Bluebook provides a Business RPM (Risk/Price Multiple) Calculator to help entrepreneurs quantify the value of their business as well as identify weak spots in need of improvement."*

ADDITIONAL REVIEWS

Fortune Small Business
Bottom Line Business
The Edward Lowe Report
Ad Agency Insider
Health & Fitness Business
American Venture
SBN Magazine
The Charlotte Observer
The Fordyce Letter
The Detroiter
Cincinnati Inquirer
Azriella Gaffe, Syn. Col
MyPrimeTime.com
Valuation Strategies.
Wisconsin Lawyer
USBX.com
PrintWear
New Page 2
Business Digest
Coaching Illustrated
The Record Reporter
Banker & Tradesman
The Honolulu Advertiser
Orange County Register

THE FORDYCE LETTER - *"A nifty little handbook."*

WICSONSIN LAWYER - *"An excellent tool for estate planners, family lawyers, and business attorneys."*

Also featured in . . .

Competitive Edge Magazine
Graphic Communications World
What's Working in Consulting
Contracting Business
Service Dealers Newsletter
The National Dipper
Giftware News
Do It Yourself Retailing
NBA Newsletter
Niche Magazine
Augusta Chronicle
Small Business Survival Center
Insurance Insight

Business Life Magazine
Independent Agent
Sandra Pesman, Syn. Col.
SNIPS Magazine
Cleaning & Restoration
HOW
KC Small Business Monthly
Ron Thomas Small Business Forum
Restaurant /Hospitality News
Pool & Spa News
Quick Service Restaurant
PalmBeachClassifieds.com

TABLE OF CONTENTS

Appendices

Business Valuation:
Use It or Lose It

AN ANSWER YOU NEED RIGHT NOW.
Business valuation is the key to cashing out with a big profit when you sell a business. It is how wealthy entrepreneurs recognize and snap-up business bargains before others notice. But you don't have to study a 600-page book to learn how to value a business. And you don't need to spend $125 on a book you don't have time to read, especially when the business of your interest might exist on Main Street not Wall Street. The Business Valuation Bluebook is the bottom line of business valuation – a solution that fits the problem.

KNOW THE NUTS AND BOLTS OF VALUATIONS.
The Business Valuation Bluebook shows you how to use valuation techniques that help you work so fast and accurately, few can argue with your conclusions. You'll learn effective phrases that help you become a negotiating sledgehammer. Real-world tips will improve your earning power whether you are a business buyer, manager or seller. They all work and are fully explained, with examples, so you can use them right away.

MAXIMIZE YOUR RETURN.
Overstating or underestimating business value by 20% or 30% can cost a business owner thousands. This book helps you avoid that costly mistake. Plus, it can help you make as much or more when you buy. For example, my first-use application of these techniques earned me $100,000! From a $1 dollar investment my first acquisition netted $50,000 cash profit in 18 months. Still another business venture,

when sold, returned a powerful $167 for every dollar invested. You can learn business valuation and work towards results like these, or, have little concept of business value and take your chances.

BUT EXERCISE CAUTION!

The material in this book is provided for information purposes only. In all cases, readers are advised to seek the advice of qualified business professionals including (but not limited to) those offering tax, legal and accounting expertise. The author, publisher and related parties involved with the development or distribution of this book and related materials assume no responsibility or liability for the consequences, good or bad, of your use of this information.

1

If You Value Your Business, You'll Value Your Business

"Most business start-ups fail. Learn valuation and buy one that didn't."

The average value of a small business often exceeds $500,000. When sold sale price variances of 5% to 20%, from $25,000 to $100,000, are common. Those who are uncertain about business value create these variances. Those who are certain about business value resolve them – to their advantage.

Many succeed at the improbable task of building a business without knowing what it is worth. This phenomenon occurs among a majority of the nearly 22 million small businesses in America today. In the details that accompany launching, buying, managing and selling companies, measuring the overall result can be forgotten. Determining the value for shares of stock, a car, a boat or a home is easy by comparison - 10 minutes of research on the Internet or a call to a broker can produce a reliable result. It isn't the same with a business. Estimates of business value are difficult to find. But measuring the wealth they create is of equal or greater importance.

The Business Valuation Bluebook offers valuation techniques that can be used by real estate and other licensed business professionals and entrepreneurs. They need solutions that are easy to learn and use that will provide reliable, accurate results, fast. Or they need professional representatives who can do so for them – appraisers, bankers, attorneys, accountants, estate planners and brokers. As the desire for self-reliance grows, however, business valuation skill becomes more important in the game of brokering, buying, selling or serving those who engage in these activities. Without knowing value it is impossible to know how much money each business venture really makes.

Types of Business Value

When reviewing literature pertaining to the world of business valuation, one thing becomes clear. Events that warrant a business valuation are frequently linked to a transfer of ownership, or its potential, in the path ahead. An entrepreneur's success or failure often depends on the ability to buy low and sell high. But how do you know where to place your bets? Those who make the most money frequently are those who best know business value.

Business valuation may be challenging because the same company can be valued several different ways to produce a variety of results. This is because a business functions on several fields of play. The estimate is influenced by the rules of each game:

✓ Estate planners value client businesses low to reduce estate taxes.

✓ Bankers value businesses low to limit risk when the business collateralizes a loan.

✓ Divorce attorneys value a business low or high depending on whom they represent.

✓ Business appraisers offer an unbiased opinion of value, but compare three appraisals on the same business. They are seldom the same.

2

✓ The IRS seems to value a business low when allowing depreciation deductions and high when it is sold (to produce a bigger capital gain).

✓ Sellers want the highest price they can get while buyers want the lowest.

Who is right and who is wrong? Values that accomplish the intended objective are accepted most often as correct, so a business can have many different values at the same time. Use of value and the quality of results produced determine what valuation estimate is best.

Not An Appraisal

Business appraisers use procedures that are more complicated than the ones presented here. Developing an appraiser's level of valuation skill can take years of effort and considerable cost. It is not surprising, then, that a good business appraiser is hard to find. The cost of an appraisal will reflect this imbalance of supply and demand, too.

Entrepreneurs do not want or need to become business appraisers. They want to make money. Developing skill at evaluating the merits of an investment and knowing what it is worth, fast, supports this goal. Years of education to learn this skill may not be a realistic option. Moreover, given the size of many small businesses that change hands, the cost of a formal business appraisal is often a bigger solution than the problem needs. A point of diminishing return is quickly reached.

Consider A Range of Values

With so many reasons to calculate value, one quickly discovers each professional has his or her own technique. With so many values available, a "value range" can be established for any business. The one appropriate for most uses will exist somewhere within the range.

Business liquidation value is at the low end of the value range and is purely market driven. This value is the price at which the property can be sold at auction.

Book value, another type, is constructed from assets and liabilities. This appears in every financial statement. Book value is considered very low, however, and seldom is recognized as an accurate representation of business market value.

At the upper limits of the value range one finds another example that is also market driven. Momentum value is generated by a popular business concept, new technologies, impressive earnings forecasts and media attention that electrify investors. The perception of value becomes greater than the value determined from financial results. Prices can soar. Just remember to ask oneself, "Did you ever try to eat a plate full of potential?"

Benchmark business values, those best suited to the entrepreneur's buying and selling activity, are derived from factors intrinsic to the business. These are cash flow, assets, returns on investment, and sales revenues. They exist in the middle of the value range and are influenced but not driven by market forces. These benchmark values take into consideration the value of intangible assets or intellectual capital, too. It is the total collection of assets deployed that builds a stream of business performance. This is extrapolated into business value using a healthy balance of objective analysis and perception.

Business intangible assets (goodwill or intellectual capital) are what many ask about when they inquire, "What is the business goodwill worth?" Goodwill is created when business performance creates value that exceeds the fair market value of tangible assets. Goodwill is usually not as great as many think, or expect, and is created from the valuation formula – not added to the result. But there are exceptions.

4

Franchise Value

One case in which a business does not even exist but can attract a value to be paid for goodwill is the franchise. There are thousands of franchise companies operating in the United States. They utilize imitative entrepreneurship to create the goodwill they sell. One needs look no farther than their record of success to confirm this fact. Franchisers sell a proven method of business operation and a uniform identity that has proven desirable to a target market. The exchange for access to these resources is called a "franchise fee." This is essentially the investment a new franchisee makes in goodwill and does not include the associated costs of starting a business: location and building improvements, furnishings, fixtures, equipment and inventory.

As a practical matter, business valuation most often occurs out of a need to facilitate a change in business ownership. This is the common ground among all who have interest in learning this skill. Accordingly, material presented throughout this text supports those professionals and entrepreneurs seeking to value businesses for this reason. Hence, the term "value" is used interchangeably with "price."

Creating A Value Range

Imagine a contest where two archers compete by aiming at a target 200 feet away. Each gets four attempts to hit the bull's eye. The one judged most accurate will be the archer who places the most arrows closest to the center of the target.

5

The competition begins, and the first archer hits the bull's eye with one shot, next misses by an inch, then misses by two or three inches with the other two. Robin Hood would be proud. The second archer misses the bull's eye first by a half-inch, then twice by 12 to 15 inches and then the final arrow fails to hit the target at all. Based on these results the first archer is clearly more accurate. He had a better aim and produced a better result. One could have more confidence in the winner, especially if he were to act as a bodyguard.

Measuring business values and the confidence we can have in them is similar to an archery contest. If values created by the capitalization, excess earnings, and both leveraged cash flow methods are all very similar, the accuracy is high. If, however, the spread of values is large, confidence in the final estimate will be less.

"Central tendency" describes the general numeric location of a group of values. The mean is the average of a group of values. The median is the value below and above which there are an equal number of values. In business valuation the mean and median are useful. In this text an example is used to illustrate how one business can be valued four different ways. Here are the results.

VALUE RANGE BELL-Quest, Ltd.	
Capitalization Method	$173,322
Excess Earnings Method	$190,782
Leveraged Cash Flow (Seller Financed)	$188,292
Leveraged Cash Flow (Bank Financed)	$178,835

A Simple Analysis

The mean of values, their average, is $182,808. This could be a good estimate of the business value.

Another approach involves use of the range and median. The Range - the distance between values at the upper and lower limits is $17,460. And the Median – one half the range added to the lowest value - is $182,052. This means no value in the range is more than $8,730 from the center of the range. That's a variance of slightly less than five percent ($8,730 ÷ $182,052) that also represents an accurate estimate of business value.

A Valuable Investment of Time

Not every valuation estimate needs to be extensive to provide a meaningful result. Indeed, the objective of this text is to reduce the time it takes to develop sensible estimates of business value. Million-dollar solutions are attractive but not necessary to produce a better result. The devil is in the details of discovery. Focused attention to this phase of valuation lays the groundwork for complex or simple valuation formulas. With good data, results from each type of valuation technique can be similar enough to be useful. The process does not have to be complicated - just effective.

Business valuation skill saves time. Like most things, regular use improves efficiency. With practice it is possible to value businesses very quickly. Of equal importance, one discovers specific pieces of information are initial indicators of value for specific types of businesses.

The ability to identify critical information and interpret it more quickly, and correctly, results in a savings of the entrepreneur's time.

A Diamond in the Rough
In a restaurant cost of goods expressed as "food cost" is important. If it is out of the range of 22% to 42%, something is amiss. Low food cost is attractive, possibly indicating a high value. High food cost is unattractive, or, it could be an opportunity in disguise – an opportunity to reduce food cost and return the savings to earnings. To discover the truth about food costs, examine three things. First, look to see if trash cans in the kitchen are full of food at the end of a business day, reduce portion size. Second, ask when prices on the menu were last changed. Food costs rise periodically; retail prices must keep pace. And finally, notice how many teenagers are employed. They often eat and give away food to their friends. All three things raise food cost. Counter-measures can lower them.

For some, valuation skill helps prevent time spent on properties not worth the attention. This is not to say all businesses don't have value. They do. Recognizing the right value is the secret. When a business is sold it includes income, assets and a marketing opportunity. The valuation process encourages a review of these things. Sometimes business income is not sufficient to justify a price that is greater than the market value of the assets. This means the business price will be based on assets. Other times there will be no income at all and no assets, but an exciting marketing opportunity. These businesses are a popular acquisition: a franchise. Recognizing that these components of value exist will help the valuation analyst target attention to discover and evaluate the source and size of business value.

Business valuation saves money. This occurs when professional representatives, brokers or entrepreneurs can estimate value themselves. The need to hire another to perform this function is eliminated. Valuations for businesses can be quite expensive.

Effective Phrase

"How did you arrive at that value?"

When the business value seems too high or low ask this question. It can completely disarm the unprepared or uninformed. If this appears to be the case, you are in a position to provide a response that will explain how value is developed and an alternative estimate. This simple strategy can win an important debate to save or earn thousands of dollars. Here's why: A solid base of logic is used to develop value. That builds confidence, which offers the strength to help one more comfortably – and favorably – resolve issues of disagreement. Assuming both parties are equally motivated to make a deal, the side with the most logical basis supporting its position usually wins. Business valuation provides this distinct advantage.

The most obvious opportunity for business valuation to have a direct (and favorable) impact on entrepreneurs' wealth is when buying or selling a business. Good valuation skill reduces the possibility a business will be sold for too much or too little. For sellers there is a lesser chance a business will be sold under the market – they save money. For buyers there is a better chance they will not pay too much for a business. "You make your money when you buy – not when you sell." In either case, business valuation helps improve the professional and financial results.

"Comps" Don't Always Compare

One doesn't have to proceed too far in a discussion of business valuation before rules of thumb from comparable sales show up. The premise, "form follows function," is used as a best defense. For example, if 10 bowling alleys sell for an average of $35,000 per lane, then the bowling center being discussed should sell for the same multiple. What if its revenue is half or double the revenue of those in the sampling from which the multiple was developed? The use of comparable sales is suddenly suspect.

Comparable business sales, otherwise known as "comps," are often regarded as a useful device to determine business value in the buying and selling game. This is very popular in the real estate business, too, where the value of a three-bedroom ranch-style home can be determined from the recently closed sale prices of similar homes in the same neighborhood. The opportunity to compare business sales, however, is limited and less reliable. Key variables affecting this valuation strategy are similarity of businesses in the sampling, number of businesses in the sampling, their location and the age of sale data.

Multiples from comparable sales have merit if they are created from businesses that are similar to the one under study. This means similar revenue, earnings, cash flows and operating management, which almost never occurs. The multiples are helpful as quick estimates of value but further investigation is required.

Size of sampling (number of comps) available to interpret business value is usually small. No two businesses are exactly alike with the same ownership, capital structure, management skill, and market characteristics. Even like-kind franchisees, that follow a proven business strategy as precisely as possible, are not equal. Further, the number of businesses qualifying as suitably similar is not large. It is difficult to capture a supply of business sales data that can be used to define consistent trends with a high degree of probability.

Location also affects the comparable sales when attempting to establish business value. To develop a larger database of comparable sales, many draw upon business sales data from other regions. Casting a wider net only means the holes in the net become larger. Data taken from markets with dissimilar economic characteristics means the businesses perform differently. This unfavorably affects the quality of the information. A frozen yogurt shop in Vail, Colorado, will fetch a higher price than the same business in Nowhere, Alaska. The "location, location, location" rule always applies and affects business value.

A third weakness in the use of comps to establish value is the age of sale data. The same motive that leads valuation consultant to seek information about sales in other locations causes them to accept information that is two, three or four years old. This type of dated information can be dangerous to use. Imagine using basic indicators of performance to value an e-commerce provider based on the companies in operation when the Internet was new. That world changed so rapidly, the value calculated would be very wrong today. Consider the effects of using comps from an area that experienced tremendous economic growth in tourism or, conversely, the layoff of thousands from major plant closings. Dated information can create inaccuracies in business value.

Comps can be helpful when their internal operating ratios are used as a device for comparison. Suppose a survey of 50 restaurants with $500,000 to $1 million in revenue reveals the average food cost is 35%. This can be helpful to determine how a restaurant under study compares – favorably or unfavorably - but it is not a direct indicator of business value. There are many sources for this type of information that can assist the analyst becoming familiar with operating characteristics of specific business types. They are not, however, strong indicators of value. Business value is better derived from existing financial barometers of performance and market characteristics. Comps may be used to help confirm the result – but not to create it.

Valuation for Do-It-Yourselfers

Most people believe business valuation techniques are difficult to learn and apply. The thickness and high cost of books on the topic tend to confirm this belief. Financial statements that provide key information only make matters worse for those with little or no exposure to accounting principles. Yet, competent business valuation is easier to learn than most realize. In fact, anyone with the ability to start, acquire, own or operate a business has all the intellectual horsepower needed. The valuation process is simple and includes four steps:

1	Collect information.
2	Interpret information.
3	Reorganize information.
4	Calculate the results.

Many discover the last step, calculating the result, is the easiest part. The first three are more difficult because they depend on the analyst's understanding and experience. With practice both improve.

2

How to Find the Diamonds
By Mining for the Facts

"Inquire to Lead"
Socrates

Study factors that create value to discover value

A report that describes the elements of a business that contribute to value is called a "Due Diligence Report" or a "due diligence." This report may be a brief summary or an extensive business review and is often accompanied by descriptive exhibits. The report will describe the strengths and weaknesses of a business. Anyone can perform a due diligence but not everyone can make it meaningful. This chapter will illustrate how it can be a constructive exercise. In general, a due diligence process has two parts: discovery and interpretation.

Boundaries of a Due Diligence

Entrepreneurs must know what they are buying, selling or trading for other property. The due diligence supports this activity. It is also useful when securing financing for expansion or planning general business strategy; both are designed to improve profit. Taken a step further, the due diligence conducted to develop a business valuation is especially meaningful. A plan to increase profits by $10,000 could increase value by $50,000 or more.

Due diligence reports are prepared by business buyers, sellers, managers, independent business consultants, business or real estate brokers, bankers, accountants, attorneys, financial planners and anyone involved in business management and - the most frequent reason a due diligence is performed - ownership transfers. Settling the question of price has major financial implications.

When conducting a due diligence, the analyst collects a variety of data describing the business and its record of performance. This is interpreted afterward and conclusions are summarized in a final report. As it may form the basis for an important decision to buy, sell or trade a business, the depth or detail of the process tends to increase in proportion to the value and commitment of money and resources.

The most frequently requested information for a due diligence precedent to a business valuation is three to five years of financial statements or tax returns. More information is also sought in follow-up requests. Following are examples of the type of materials often collected for the business valuation due diligence:

✓ Company identification

✓ Ownership structure w/shareholder agreements

✓ Business location and contact points

✓ Description of business activity

✓ Summary of trailing revenue, expenses and earnings

✓ Statement of the business capital structure (assets, liabilities, etc.)

✓ List of business assets

✓ Market position of the business

✓ Description of products and services offered

14

✓ Characteristics of the workforce

✓ Marketing opportunities within reach

✓ Photographs, maps and descriptions of premises and key equipment

✓ Location analysis

✓ Competitive market analysis

✓ A multi-year forecast of business financial results

Collecting information for the due diligence report occurs through a series of meetings with business principals. They or their appointed representatives work closely with the analyst. These meetings expedite the due diligence/valuation process. Serious investors leave no stone unturned in their inquiries. Good information helps reduce uncertainty and reduce business risk. If transactions become lengthy, updates to the due diligence are often requested.

Performing a due diligence for a small business valued under $5 million can be difficult. Information requested is private – not public – so access has always been strictly limited. Company contacts occur directly with business principals whose sense of exposure is professional and personal. Sensitive information inadvertently released to competitors or the wrong people can cause serious damage to business performance. Financial statements are a grade card of management performance and may reveal unsatisfactory marks, therefore, it is natural for business owners to enter a due diligence with skepticism and concern.

Business owners are often unwilling to disclose financial details about their business because they feel threatened. Here are actions to build trust so they will be more forthcoming with important details for the due diligence.

✓ "Spit & Whittle" first

✓ Explain the benefits of a due diligence

✓ Describe how the due diligence is performed

✓ Ask easy, non-threatening questions first

✓ Remind the owner of their objectives

✓ Listen more than talk

✓ Offer to execute a Non-Disclosure Agreement

Non-Disclosure Agreements

Non-disclosure agreements are written promises not to disclose confidential information about a business making such disclosures. General business information not considered sensitive or damaging may be released prior to execution of a non-disclosure agreement, however, the formal due diligence process begins after a non-disclosure is in place.

Those interested in learning more about a specific business – buyers, brokers, accountants, lawyers, bankers, etc. – give a non-disclosure or confidentiality agreement to the business owners. It is a normal and appropriate procedure, necessary because maintaining secrecy while conducting a due diligence is imperative to all concerned.

Non-disclosure agreements permit interested parties to quickly establish their legitimacy, discretion and reliability with business principals. It is a counterpoint to a seller's release of financial information as an indication of serious intent. Non-disclosure agreements are convenient vehicles to handle this issue briskly and with dexterity.

Non-disclosure agreements are no guarantee of secrecy, however. Unfortunately, business principals themselves are often the source of information leaks. Innocent conversations with an employee, spouse or business associate may contain references that appear harmless but could be explosive. Once out of the ownership loop, "inside" information gets reinterpreted and can travel exceptionally fast. The mere mention that a due diligence is occurring may be enough to set imaginations and rumors in motion. These can demoralize employees and drive off customers. Conscientious attention to this issue by *all* parties is required to preserve confidentiality.

Non-disclosure agreements come in many forms. Some are literally an analyst's one-sentence promise not to tell what he or she learns. Others are pages of detailed instructions that converge at the point of remedies. These are threats to be carried out if the promises kept are broken. Non-disclosure agreements typically include the following elements:

✓ Name of the party giving the promise (often names the analyst conducting the due diligence and the clients if any)

✓ Name of the party receiving the promise

✓ Statement of the confidentiality promise: explains what the analyst promises to retain as confidential; i.e. types and formats of information released. Sometimes this is added as an exhibit to ensure that specific areas are covered by the agreement while others remain off limits. For example, material pertaining to financial performance is available while material pertaining to product development is not. The decision to exclude certain information is most often governed by the intended use of the due diligence investigation.

✓ Limitations on use of information received: states the purpose for receiving privileged information. The agreement may include a statement defining who, in addition to the analyst, may have access to information disclosed. If third-party advisers - a client, supervisor, accountant, banker, attorney, business consultant, investor or other professional representative – are involved, they may be asked to execute a separate but similar agreement. This will occur prior to receipt of any privileged information.

✓ Breach of agreement: defines acts that constitute a breach of the agreement – generally unauthorized releases of confidential material.

✓ Remedies for breach of agreement: typically grant the party receiving the confidentiality agreement the legal right to secure relief and compensation from the analyst. A remedy may include a provision for a restraining order and/or court injunction to prevent further release of potentially injurious information. It could also address the penalties for breach of the agreement that, in some cases, can include court costs to secure prevention of further release; cash penalties; or any other remedy legal counsel for the damaged party chooses to pursue in addition to court and legal costs of collection.

✓ Term (normally ties expiration to a date set after the due diligence is completed; one to two years is not uncommon)

✓ Signature and date

Failure to Disclose Is a Deal-Killer

In some cases, despite the existence of a fully executed confidentiality agreement, business principals may elect to withhold certain information requested. This may be ownership's prerogative. Confidentiality agreements do not necessarily grant the analyst rights to demand information; they grant business principals the right to take legal action if information disclosed is not kept confidential. Still, failing to disclose relevant information can be a warning flag. It may also be counterproductive, as it prevents the analyst from conducting a due diligence in advance of a business valuation. Worse, it often creates suspicion that business principals are attempting to cover up problematic issues. Business buyers or their representatives will usually withdraw their interest when information is withheld.

Effective Phrase

"Would you ever buy a business sight unseen?"

This is a formidable response to the owner that says, "Bring me an offer and I'll show you my books." This frequently heard statement is a common response among owners threatened by inquiries about their business. Developing a meaningful business value without data, however, forces the valuation consultant to work blindfolded – an unrealistic expectation.

The primary asset purchased with a business is usually the stream of income. Without financial records to describe it, neither broker nor buyer can know what is offered. The broker attempting to represent a property with undocumented benefits is playing a high-risk game. Any investor attempting to buy it is exposed to high levels of uncertainty. Both make commitments of time and money to investigate a risk-filled venture without knowing if initial interest or effort is justified. Neither can calculate an initial estimate of value based on fact.

Perhaps more importantly, accountants or attorneys cannot properly advise the parties as to the size and scope of business implications created by a business transaction without detailed disclosures. Neither will bankers consider financing any kind of business without financial disclosures to justify and assure repayment of debt is plausible. The ability to repay from business earnings must be clear and unquestionable. This is only possible when financial disclosures (limited while still revealing enough to engender increased interest) are made at the appropriate time – before the offer is made.

The non-disclosure agreement is a precedent to a due diligence. This comes before an offer to purchase a business that spells out the conditions of a sale. A contract contingency to permit more detailed disclosures after acceptance of an initial offer is the norm. Experienced brokers perform their due diligence when listing a property in anticipation of questions and inquiries that will follow. They know a client's follow-up investigation will occur to confirm the specifics of representations.

Business owners who fail to disclose necessary information as part of a due diligence investigation are shortsighted. They immediately disqualify knowledgeable and capable players. The price paid is very often a business that does not sell, becomes shop-worn or becomes known as "on the market" over time. It can be weakened by competitors and eventually lose customers and business revenue. Ownership burnout often occurs, as well. The final outcome may be liquidation for pennies on the dollar. Sadly, with a good due diligence/business valuation and reasonable expectations, such a business might have sold earlier for a profit.

Ensure business principals are cooperative and forthcoming with information needed by adding a failure to disclose provision to the confidentiality agreement. As a result, requested materials are easier to collect. If materials are not forthcoming, the analyst may be released from any continuing obligation to perform services.

Organizing a Due Diligence

Knowing what to ask for, when to ask for it and how to organize information will make a due diligence easier and more productive. It is helpful to recall two premises that prompt the effort: 1) Is information related to a specific event? (Does someone want to buy, sell, trade or refinance the business?) and 2) Is the due diligence related to a specific time? (How much time is going to be available to complete the task?)

Suppose owners of a restaurant were interested in financing to expand the kitchen production capacity – an event. Indicators needed for a quick feasibility estimate might include the following:

✓ Financial statements

✓ Existing mortgages or liens

✓ Leases for equipment and the location

✓ Current equipment list with descriptions of major machinery

✓ A three-year revenue/earnings forecast

This should be sufficient to construct a preliminary cost/benefit assessment of the proposed expansion strategy. If favorable, a more complete due diligence may be performed. From that, changes in business value may be estimated to measure the total benefit of the expansion plan. Sometimes adding $10,000 to earnings creates an additional $50,000 of business value – equity. Keep this in mind. Bankers want to know how much additional profit is created, but business valuation skill permits the entrepreneur to go farther by estimating wealth created through refinancing to support expansion.

Expect the Unexpected

The opportunity to buy or sell a business is frequently unexpected. For this reason time is a factor when information to value the business is needed quickly. Perhaps an opportunity to acquire a competitor or accept an unsolicited offer is in play. The more likely approach to a due diligence in this case will begin with an all-out document dump. Everything comes at once and it is the analyst's job to quickly organize, prioritize and produce meaningful results.

The value of regular business valuations when opportunity comes unexpectedly cannot be overstated. The ability to act fast (with homework already in place) provides a competitive advantage.

To simplify the reporting process, data may be prioritized in categories. This divides discovery into steps that match the results needed with the time and energy expended to develop them.

Follow receipt of initial indicators of business performance by requesting other key variables and strings of more detailed data. This would be priority types of information from other categories within the due diligence inquiry. For example, food cost information is more meaningful when combined with traffic count at the existing location, seating capacity and service style, market position, promotional tactics, age of kitchen and equipment and menu selections. One or two descriptive sentences for each is often enough to determine if the property is worth a closer look. If the initial impressions are not attractive move on, wasting little time.

Here's a helpful shortcut. Restaurateurs are acutely aware of *"food cost"* (i.e., the cost of food purchased expressed as a percent of gross income). This data item offers a quick indicator of gross profitability. If the figure is low, management probably runs a tight ship; too high and there are probably old prices on the menu, excessive waste in the garbage at day's end, or theft. This single measurement device provides valuable clues to the restaurant's overall operating efficiency. Determine this percentage of revenue first.

Checklists Lead to the Next Step

To organize and prioritize information efficiently the following checklists (covering Finance, Control, Marketing, Sales, Production and Service) may be helpful. The categories are common to all businesses, and the information listed can be selected on a case-by-case basis. Asterisked (*) items are most important; they help form a good early impression of the business with less due diligence. For convenience these are located in the appendix.

> The Sergeant Said
> *To see your target in the dark,*
> *It often helps to set your mark*
> *In line of sight just to the right:*
> *Then your bulls-eye comes to light.*
>   *Warren Lane Molton*

3

Accurate Variables Produce Reliable Values

"Good data leads to good results."

Recognizing and developing variables needed to value a business is an essential skill. It is possible with business financial records that are the source of most data retrieved from a due diligence. Always use data from the past three to five years. Selected information catches the eye of the business valuation consultant. Some data will be used in their original form while others are reconstituted for greater meaning. When accurately extracted, developed and introduced into valuation formulas they can create reliable business values.

Business Balance Sheet

A financial statement uses numbers to describe the business capital structure. The financial statement has two basic parts: the balance sheet, which includes a list of business assets and liabilities (essence of the capital structure) and the operating statement, which is a record of business revenue, expenses and earnings. Consider the balance sheet.

Assets

The first variables to know describe the value of assets included in a business. The two measures of asset value to identify are book value of assets and their market value. Both are affected, increased or decreased, by several factors.

A list of assets appears in the first or top section of the balance sheet. Assets are divided into two categories. These are current assets that include such things as cash-on-hand, accounts receivable, prepaid expenses, certain types of equipment, and inventory. The second category includes larger items such as land and buildings, which are considered fixed assets.

The value assigned to each asset listed is taken from its original cost when placed in service (acquired for use by the business). Also listed is an entry called "accumulated depreciation." This is a deduction representing a loss of asset value resulting from normal wear-and-tear in use. The amount of depreciation taken is subtracted from the asset's original cost. Asset values and accumulated depreciation are often grouped together for simplicity. The difference between original cost of assets and depreciation subtracted is the "book" value of business assets – their value as they appear in the business books.

Effective Phrase

"You get income, assets and a marketing opportunity."

Say this when a buyer asks, "If I buy this business what do I get for my money?" It's a short response that opens the door for arguments designed to justify business value. Many of the benefits of business ownership are intangible. But these fall short of the inquiry of the steely-eyed buyer preparing to write a check. Most want to know they are acquiring "tangible" assets in exchange for cash. They are, in fact, acquiring both tangibles and intangibles.

Tangible Vs. Intangible Assets

Frequently assets listed in a financial statement are only tangible – property one can touch and feel. Typically, intangible assets are not included in the asset variable used to value the business. They differ because they cannot be touched or directly felt. Likewise, banks do not accept intangible assets as collateral for financing. Exceptions may occur, however, when intangible assets are directly connected to revenue creation. Patents, copyrights, secret formulas or production processes are common examples. These can be listed in the balance sheet summary of assets. The final estimate of asset value will be used in the excess earnings and leveraged cash flow formulas presented in chapters dealing with those valuation techniques.

Goodwill

In some cases goodwill is listed as an intangible asset. Confusion may surround the meaning of "goodwill" when the term is used to represent value in a business. In many cases an investor, acting on advice of a professional representative, will refuse to pay for goodwill as a part of the business price. The implication is goodwill is intangible, therefore, conveying nothing of value and not a fair exchange for cash or property. The real intent, though, may be to avoid allocating any portion of the purchase price to goodwill. This is because goodwill according to the Internal Revenue Code is amortized in a particular manner. It offers limited tax benefits compared to other assets with shorter, or more favorable, depreciation or amortization periods.

27

Effective Phrase

"Goodwill is the excess of purchase price for a business over the market value of its tangible assets."

This is the quick response to the often-asked question, "What's my goodwill worth." The response is provided by the Internal Revenue Code. It's a deflection from a more meaningful response but one that is necessary. It is not possible to estimate the value of goodwill without estimating the value of the business.

This approach buys time and shifts the discussion to the need for more information. Use it as an opportunity to explain why a simple due diligence (review of financial records) is needed. Explain that goodwill is not valued separately from the business, or without the total business value. Instead, value the business first, subtract the value of tangibles and the remainder is the intangibles – goodwill (to their way of thinking). Close the discussion with "I'll be happy to estimate the value of your goodwill once I estimate the value of your business."

Where goodwill is justifiable, it is not difficult to illustrate its value. Compare the cost to buy the benefits of goodwill (revenue, earnings, reputation, location, market position, procedures and product/service mix) with the investment required to build it (and the accompanying benefits) from scratch. Also, consider the time it takes to buy versus build. Keep in mind the risk to a start-up business is often much greater than the risk of failure in a business already performing successfully. Sometimes buying goodwill is a good deal.

Obsolescence

This term indicates an asset, service or product is becoming obsolete and losing its value. It is important to recognize obsolescence because it will affect, favorably or unfavorably, the value of business assets. Old inventory not suitable for resale, for example, or equipment no longer in use might be discounted (perhaps below book value) when attempting to estimate tangible business asset values. Two kinds of obsolescence are important to consider.

Functional obsolescence occurs when the need or demand for an asset ceases to exist. For example, printing presses will become obsolete as demand for documents transmitted via email and the Internet grows. Newspapers and magazines are published electronically. This eliminates the cost of paper, printing and shipping, offering publishers a significant savings of manpower, time and money. The increased speed of production shortens the information cycle so the product timeliness and desirability improves, too. Books published directly on the Internet will contribute further to the growing obsolescence of printing presses.

Economic obsolescence is another way assets become obsolete. This often occurs in tandem with its functional cousin. Declining demand for older computer microprocessors is related to new software that would only run on faster, more powerful chips (functional obsolescence). Consequently, sales and the economic value of older chips are constantly being eliminated. This is economic obsolescence.

Economic obsolescence may also occur independently, however. A good example is found in a business's heating and cooling system (HVAC). Significant improvements of energy efficiencies in HVAC equipment have occurred in the past decade. Compared to old systems, new units do a better job managing air in the workplace environment. They also create savings, permitting their cost to be recovered in a few years. As a result, many business owners discover that, while still functional, old systems are too expensive to operate. Economic obsolescence has occurred and the value of the affected equipment is reduced.

In some instances appreciation will cause an asset's value to exceed its book value. Simple marketplace growth is a common reason. A building might have appreciated in value because of market trends even though it is being depreciated for tax purposes. Real estate values in good locations usually rise. Thus, original cost and book values are lower than the price investors would pay to acquire such a resource. In the alternative, an accelerated depreciation schedule may outpace the useful life of an asset to create a similar disparity between book and economic value.

Appreciation may also occur when an asset value can be increased due to a unique/specific function - its highest and best use. For example, mobile home communities often purchase and rent used mobile homes. These are aggressively depreciated but can remain useful for many years. Suppose the rent collectable is $350 per month. Using the Capitalization method of business valuation and a 50% rate of return, the economic value of a single mobile home rental might be $8,400. The book value, however, could be zero.

Because the book value of each asset can be affected by functional or economic obsolescence, or appreciation, making appropriate adjustments in asset values improves accuracy of the business valuation estimate.

Market & Replacement Value

Market value is the amount one could reasonably expect to pay for an asset. It may be synonymous with replacement value or the cost to replace an asset with another of like kind. Neither reflects a property's book value nor its original cost – they usually lie somewhere between the two. It may be difficult to develop a value estimate in which all agree. Use original cost, book value, appraisals (if available) and discussions with ownership or knowledgeable industry professionals to develop a reasonable estimate of market or replacement asset values. More cooks will not spoil the stew.

When all is said and done, lenders tend to rely on book value as the basis for conservative loan approvals. Sellers want to use original or current economic value to raise the business price. Buyers try to use economic value to borrow and book value to buy. The analyst's job is to develop a complete set of defensible key variables, including book, market and replacement asset values. It will be used in the valuation formulas.

Liabilities

Following the list of assets on a balance sheet is a list of the business's debts, or liabilities. These are categorized as current or long-term. The former includes obligations such as accounts payable, operating lines of credit due within 90 days, accrued vacation pay, and so on. The latter typically includes loans secured to purchase the business, related property and equipment, or major capital improvements. Sometimes loans to shareholders will appear in this section. The current and long-term liabilities are combined to indicate the total liabilities of a business.

Equity

Subtracting existing debt from the net value of capital and property (which in some cases includes intellectual capital) contributed to an investment yields the equity amount. Ownership equity in an acquisition is usually the down payment used to acquire a business. This is called "hard" equity because it represents a commitment of physical resources (e.g. cash). This does not always occur in a business acquisition, however. Some businesses are purchased wholly with borrowed funds, so there is no equity.

How, then, can equity be created where there is no original investment? Four forces combine to produce equity: income, tax benefits, amortization and appreciation.

√ **Income** - Without spending a dime for equity, it is possible to get a job and make a living wage. Ownership of a business should offer this, too, or the investment is questionable.

√ **Tax Benefits** - Businesses have the potential to offer tax savings on earnings compared with the same earnings provided by a job. Some businesses have deductions that reduce the earnings they create. The effect is to reduce taxable earnings and tax liability but not necessarily cash flow. Consequently, employment and business earnings could be the same, but the latter might be taxed at a lower marginal rate. A tax savings can be the result.

√ **Amortization** - Business ownership can be like an investment savings account. With reasonable financial leverage and effective management, payment on debt comes from business earnings. A portion of each payment

32

on the debt is credited to interest on the outstanding loan: the remainder retires the principal until the debt is fully paid. Each principal payment represents a reduction in debt and, provided the business has not declined in value, a corresponding increase in ownership equity.

√ **Appreciation** - When a business appreciates, its value grows. Business revenue and earnings increase because of effective management, favorable market forces and a variety of other reasons. Normally increases in earnings are translated into greater business value, and the increase becomes added equity for ownership.

The combination of income, tax benefits, amortization and appreciation has an effect on ownership equity similar to compounding. Many underestimate the total effect magnified by an improved ability to buy low and sell high.

In addition to hard equity, there is another type called "sweat equity" – created by entrepreneurs with the management skill to run a business successfully. If the business grows in value, additional equity is the result. Management entrepreneurs can receive stock or ownership in lieu of a portion of their salary or in the place of bonuses. This is normal and accompanied by performance measurements to ensure stock is not given freely. Unlike hard equity, this form comes from a commitment of time, talent and energy. It can provide a convenient way for entrepreneurs to acquire a business interest with nothing down.

The amount of equity in a business can affect its value. Businesses with little or no debt are sometimes perceived as more stable and secure. Absence of debt suggests a business that can withstand changes in sales cycles, capitalize on unexpected market opportunities, compensate employees well and show little or no deferred maintenance or obsolescence in furnishings and equipment. This perception of security may generate a premium value compared to businesses burdened by heavy debt – provided the absence of debt is not accompanied by a sense of complacency on the part of management.

Sometimes a section of the balance sheet shows a reconciliation of *stockholder* or *owner's equity*. This is not the same as the business's value. It is also not a measurement of equity based on the business value estimate but, instead, is benchmarked against the book value. (Business book value is the book value of all assets minus liabilities.)

Generally, owner's equity is a function of cash paid for the business or stock in the company, additional cash paid into the company, and earnings that have been allowed to remain in the business (called *retained earnings*). The owner's equity portion of the balance sheet also describes the amount of stock the company is authorized to issue, the par (nominal or face) value of each share, and the number of shares outstanding.

> **"**In business, numbers are the symbols by which you measure the various activities of an individual enterprise. They are not the business; they are only pictures of the business. Numbers serve as a sort of thermometer which measures the health and well-being of the enterprise.**"**
>
> *Hal Geneen*

Penetrating the persona of a business through its numbers improves understanding of business capacity, problems and potential.

BALANCE SHEET
BELL-Quest, Ltd.

Assets
CURRENT ASSETS

Inventory at Cost	$ 55,000.00
Accounts Receivable	13,498.41
Prepaid Expenses	2,401.08
Security Deposits	675.00
Cash in Accounts	19,904.66
Furnishings and Equipment	15,000.00
Accumulated Depreciation	<15,000.00>
Net Current Assets	$ 91,479.15

FIXED ASSETS

Land @ Cost	$ 7,500.00
Building	80,000.00
Accumulated Depreciation	<29,333.00>
Net Building	50,667.00
Intangibles and good will	25,000.00
Accumulated Amortization	<18,333.00>
Net Intangibles and good will	6,667.00
Net Fixed Assets	$ 64,834.00
TOTAL ASSETS	$156,313.15

Liabilities
CURRENT LIABILITIES

Accounts Payable	$ 33,127.50
Expenses Due	7,638.00
Operating Credit Line	0.00
Employee Benefits/Taxes Payable	542.88
Total Current Liabilities	$ 41,308.38

LONG TERM LIABILITIES

Bank Loan on Business	$ 49,323.13
TOTAL LIABILTIES	90,631.51
OWNERSHIP EQUITY	65,681.64
TOTAL LIABILITIES AND EQUITY	$156,313.15

4

Cash Flow Analysis
For the Math Impaired

The 80/20 Rule
80% of sales are made by 20% of the people.
80% of success comes from 20% of the effort.
You already know 80% of how to value a business.
Here's the other 20%.

Completing a business valuation formula isn't rocket science. Simple math skills are often enough. For a small investment of effort to learn this technique, a major advance in ability can be achieved.

Profit & Loss Statement

The second part of the financial statement describes business revenue, expenses, and profit or loss created from operations. This document provides the most important data needed to develop a coherent business value.

There are many names for a summary of a business's record of financial performance: "Books," "Profit and Loss Report," "Operating Statement," "EOY (End-of-Year) Results," "P & L," and "Income Summary" are a few. In general, they offer a description of the business results for the current and previous years.

How to Proceed

To construct a business valuation, copy data from this section of the financial statement onto a standard form

Profit & Loss Statement. This is a detailed but valuable exercise. When copying data the entrepreneur's attention is directed to each entry. Besides speeding up familiarity with the business, it also will prompt important questions for management to consider such as, "How was [an expense] created?" or "Why is [an item] increasing or decreasing?" and "Is [a certain expense] necessary to operate the business?" Asking such questions prior to performing a valuation exercise frequently unearths new data to offer a clearer picture of the business's earning power.

Placing financial data into a familiar format has other benefits, too. Familiarity reduces difficulty. This is important since business financial statements are constructed in a variety of formats. Using the same format with each new analysis makes the job easier. In addition, forms presented in this text highlight key data linked to valuation formulas that follow. When transferring data to the analyst's forms, certain items will appear that are common to most businesses. A discussion of those items follows.

Revenue

Revenue is created by the sale of a business's products or services. Gross income does not include revenue from sources unrelated to the principal business activity. (e.g., interest on bank deposits owned by the business, earnings or rents from investments made and owned by the business, etc.). Observe the trend of revenue during previous years, taking note of significant increases or decreases. Attempt to correlate trends with specific events related to management or the marketplace – therein lies the reason they may have occurred, providing valuable insight into business planning.

Cost of Goods

"Cost of goods" represents the total wholesale cost of merchandise purchased or produced for resale. In retailing, distributing or wholesaling, business items purchased are sold at a higher price. In a restaurant, cost of goods is often referred to as "food cost" or the cost of bulk food purchased to produce the meals served. Manufacturing businesses include the cost of raw materials and labor required to build the finished product in their cost of goods calculations.

Calculate cost of goods by subtracting from revenue the cost of all merchandise purchased during the year. Take a second step and examine cost of goods as a percent of revenue; this can be revealing. In times of increasing business activity, cost of goods as a percent of revenue might remain fixed or decrease slightly. Increases in the percent of cost of goods may accompany declining revenues – business might be slow. Inventory taken for owners' use is another reason cost of goods could increase. Anticipation of a business sale is another. Poor cash flows that restrict the ability to maintain inventory at optimum levels also accompany falling revenues.

Gross Profit

This is revenue left after cost of goods has been subtracted. When calculating a product's retail price from its wholesale cost, the percent of markup is added to the wholesale price. Suppose an item costs ten dollars ($10.00) and the markup for resale is 50%. One would take 50% of $10.00 ($5.00) and add it to the cost of the product ($10.00), resulting in a sales price of $15.00. But notice, although the markup is 50% the gross margin (gross profit when stated as a percent of the retail price instead of wholesale cost) is 33%. The latter percentage is calculated by dividing the resale price into the amount of markup ($5÷$15). It is important to differentiate between markup and margin in conversation. Here's why:

A Shortcut To Cash Flow

Occasionally it is necessary to quickly size up a business without the benefit of financial records. This occurs when a broker is attempting to list a business or when an entrepreneur is casually investigating a business he or she may want to buy. Even though the books are not available, many sellers are still willing to have a casual conversation. A little information can be very revealing for those who adopt this ingenious approach.

A first impression of business profitability can be created from three simple, non-threatening questions:

1. What is the average revenue per month?
2. What is the average markup on merchandise or services?
3. What are the average operating costs per month?

Divide the average monthly revenue by 1 + the percent of markup on merchandise sold. The answer is the cost of goods per month. Subtract this amount from revenue to determine gross profit. Subtract monthly expenses from gross profit. The answer is an estimate of business cash flow. Here's how it works with numbers:

Assume sales are $50,000 per month and merchandise is marked up an average of 30%. Cost of goods = $50,000÷130% = $38,461.54. Gross profit is $50,000 - $38,461.54 = $11,538.46. Estimated cash expenses to run the business are $6,000 per month. So the estimated cash flow is $11,538.46 - $6,000, or $5,538.46 per month and the annual cash flow is $66,461.53.

Now the analyst can determine if the business's earning power justifies continued interest. If so, the due diligence that follows will attempt to confirm these initial conclusions.

Another situation occurs in which understanding ways to calculate gross revenue from cost of goods, and the inverse, is helpful. This is when taking a business inventory prior to the sale of a company. It is necessary to determine how much inventory is present and included in the sale price. The physical inventory is typically taken by an outside inventory service that counts all the merchandise based on retail price. This method is faster than checking thousands of items against their original invoiced costs.

A Shortcut to the Closing Table

Suppose, for the sell-out exercise, inventory is marked up 30% and has a retail value of $75,000. By subtracting 30% from $75,000, the indicated wholesale value could be $52,500. This, however, is an incorrect approach to the valuation of the inventory. Thirty percent of the expected resale price is more than 30% of the actual cost. The actual wholesale value is $57,692, or $5,192 more. This is because the retail value is 130% of the cost of goods. Therefore, when the retail value ($75,000) is divided by 130%, the actual wholesale value of the inventory is $57,692.31.

Operating Expenses

All the costs of running a business are the business expenses. They include insurance, payroll, depreciation, interest, maintenance, rent, office supplies, freight, automobile and travel expenses, and so forth. Keep two things in mind when reviewing a business's record of expenses.

"You can't save yourself into prosperity." Tom Woods, former Chief Financial Officer of TWA notes this when responding to management preoccupied with cost cutting strategies. Frugality may be a virtue but it is possible to take a good thing too far. Cost cutting, in the extreme, translates into declining production capacity and the ability to serve demands from existing and potential customers. Thus begins a vicious cycle. Reductions in expenses are not too difficult to make. They will, however, increase the workload and stress on existing employees and resources needed to fill the gap they create. If not restored to previous levels, production and service may decline. Sales will likely decrease. This causes more expense reductions, which is the cycle renewing itself in a business that is slowly bleeding to death.

A classic example of this scenario occurs when the budget axe hits marketing and advertising budgets in response to poor revenue performance. Revenue and brand awareness go hand in hand. Indeed, in these days of electronic commerce the "brand" floating in cyberspace is often all the customer knows. So market awareness and revenue have become inseparable. It is good to remember that cutting expenses is a short-term fix and a finite strategy to improve profitability. Keeping the focus on ways to increase revenue has infinite possibilities and, though painful in the short term, can insure long-term prosperity.

The second characteristic of expenses is that business owners intentionally maximize them to minimize earnings and tax liability. Therefore, a thorough review of expenses is a valuable prerequisite to the business valuation steps. Upon review, expenses, not skimming, can be a source of cash flow not readily apparent in the business Net Profit.

Net Profit

Subtracting expenses from gross profit calculates earnings, known as "net profit", "net operating income," "NOI," "profit," "taxable income," or simply "earnings" and so on. Typically, net profit is stated after depreciation, amortization and interest, as well as all other business expenses, are deducted.

In conversation with others, it is important to define precisely what net profit really means. Different people have a different idea and confusion can be costly. When allowed to continue, such misunderstandings can hinder the valuation process and negatively affect its intended use thereafter.

Earnings Summary

An earnings summary is a short form of the business operating (income and expense) statement. It will include the basic key variables just mentioned: gross revenue, cost of goods, gross profit, expenses and net profit.

EARNINGS SUMMARY BELL-Quest, Ltd.	
Revenue	$ 608,951.00
Cost of Goods	<397,530.00>
Gross Profit	211,421.00
Expenses	<189,501.29>
Net Profit	21,919.71

These, or variants of each, appear in most business operating statements. The earnings summary helps simplify the problem of becoming acquainted quickly with a business operating statement. Look for the earnings summary to simplify the investigation.

Trailing Earnings

Trailing earnings are earnings recorded during pervious years of business operation. These are important because they represent the rock-hard reality of a business's performance – not its potential. Valuations are more often based on trailing earnings and not a forecast of blazing success. Remember, history remains the best predictor of future performance. Consider three to five years of trailing earnings when constructing a business value estimate.

Examining trailing earnings is also important because businesses are in a constant state of change. Creating business value from one year of performance does not take into consideration business trends. These could be highly favorable or unfavorable, thereby affecting business value; so, effective valuations use trailing earnings as a way to introduce the influence of trends into estimates of business value. For the sophisticated entrepreneur, trailing earnings trends provide the basis for forecasting future earnings. For most, however, trailing earnings are useful to weight cash flows that already exist and influence variables used in creating a risk/price multiple, described in the next chapter. Study the Operating Statement that follows.

PROFIT & LOSS STATEMENT
BELL-Quest, Ltd.
January 1 thru December 31

REVENUE	
Gross Sales	$581,282.00
Service Income	27,669.00
Total Revenue	$608,951.00
COST OF GOODS	
Merchandise Purchases	$376,778.25
Labor on Service	$ 20,751.75
Total Cost of Goods	<$397,530.00>
GROSS PROFIT	$211,421.00
EXPENSES	
Advertising	35,913.50
Amortization	1,667.66
Auto & Truck	332.00
Commissions	6,187.12
Depreciation	4,809.00
Dues & Subscriptions	179.00
Entertainment	1,776.00
Freight	11,378.60
Insurance	2,835.00
Interest	4,533.29
Janitorial	3,882.00
Laundry & Uniforms	900.00
Licenses	75.00
Non-Recurring Expenses	501.66
Payroll	61,871.22
Payroll Taxes	4,604.34
Professional Fees	900.00
Real Estate Taxes	5,743.00
Repairs & Maintenance	2,700.00
Salaries (Owner's)	18,000.00
Supplies Office	421.00
Travel	1,487.53
Telephone	2,964.00
Utilities	12,828.00
Other	3,012.37
Total Expenses	$ 189,501.29
NET PROFIT	$ 21,919.71

5

The Difference Between
Net Profit and Cash Flow

**"It's not what you make –
it's what you keep that matters most."**

The variables used in valuation formulas are retrieved from the due diligence performed. These variables are not particularly difficult to develop, but maintaining accuracy is very important. For example, cash flow is the base variable from which the valuation estimate is built. If it is incorrect, valuation estimates can be equally off the mark. Take great care when building these indicators of value. Small adjustments may correctly or incorrectly magnify the outcome.

Net Profit Versus Cash Flow
Recall obsolescence affects the value of business assets. Depending on the particular situation, an asset could be worth more or less than its book value. The entrepreneur conducting a business valuation needs to adjust asset values to account for obsolescence that may have occurred. Similarly, an earnings reconstruction (ERCON) resolves discrepancies between apparent and actual business earnings. To do this add expenses [to the net profit] of the current owner that will not exist or be different for a new owner.

The ERCON is performed after the analyst has become familiar with the business's financial statements. With the

ERCON, key variables may be developed: EBIT, EBITDA, cash flow and weighted cash flow. The latter is used in the capitalization, excess earnings and leveraged cash flow methods of business valuation. These will be discussed in later chapters.

An ERCON is necessary because business owners frequently maximize expenses to minimize earnings. This is a strategy of tax avoidance used to limit taxable earnings so tax liability may be reduced. It is also a catch-22. To the untrained or inexperienced, the business net profit may not seem appealing and makes a business investment less attractive. This situation is the real reason most owners resist financial disclosures to potential buyers of their business.

Simply put, business net profit will seldom justify a realistic business value compared to those derived from business cash flow or free cash flow. An owner knows the difference between what is reported for tax purposes and what he or she actually gets to keep. Explaining it to a buyer is a challenge. But when access to financial details of a business is denied, an ERCON and subsequent valuations cannot be completed. So, ownership's tax avoidance strategy becomes an albatross around their neck. It can prevent them from adequate justifications of value. This is the valuation consultant's opportunity. Resolving the issue enables parties involved to see clearly how a selected business value can be justified. EBIT and EBITDA are popular examples of variables produced using the simplest type of ERCON. Many business professionals regularly use these terms.

EBIT & EBITDA

EBIT is an acronym that means Earnings Before Interest and Taxes. In this case earnings is synonymous with net profit. To calculate EBIT add the business's interest expense to the net profit. If income taxes are treated as an expense or a deduction before net profit is calculated, add it, too. Note, however, these types of taxes are normally subtracted after net profit is calculated. When one or both of these costs are added to net profit the resulting value called EBIT is the result.

EBITDA is an extension of EBIT. It includes two additional items that may appear in business expenses. These are Depreciation and Amortization. These values may be added to the net profit because no cash is paid out for depreciation or amortization. The acronym therefore represents Earnings Before Income Taxes, Depreciation & Amortization.

The IRS takes the position that investments in tangible and certain intangible assets may be recovered over time by the taxpayer. The vehicle used to accomplish this is a prorated share of their original value charged as an expense to the business operation. This is a substitute for treating the original cost as an expense in the first year the asset was acquired. Consequently, since the original cost was paid in the beginning the amount expensed each year does not represent cash paid out. It is, therefore, a deduction only and may be added back to EBIT. The resulting macro variable, EBITDA, is often considered a more accurate reflection of business earnings available to ownership. The variance between net profit and cash flow grows.

Depreciation

Certain assets used in the production of business income can be deducted from gross revenue either directly or indirectly. This is how the Internal Revenue Service enables business owners to recover the cost of assets purchased by the business, hence the alternative name - "cost recovery."

Direct expense deductions include cost of goods, rent and other perishables such as office supplies. Indirect deductions occur when an asset's useful life extends beyond a typical business period (one year). In these cases a portion of the asset's value is deducted each year to represent the eventual wasting of the asset that occurs. When fully depreciated an asset's book value can be zero. To determine the actual amount of depreciation that can be taken check current IRC regulations.

Some assets cannot be depreciated. Personal assets, a home or a car not used for business are examples. Other assets with an indefinite life, such as land, are not depreciated either.

Amortization

Amortization is the depreciation of intangible assets. It appears as a deduction in the expense section of a business operating statement. Unlike their tangible counterparts, intangible assets are amortized according to a different schedule. The typical amortization period is 15 years – straight line. In all cases, check the current IRC regulations for rules regarding use of amortization.

In the past the IRC has indicated amortization applies to assets acquired by the business that are actively used to produce income. It does not indicate intangibles created by the business can be amortized. However, in certain cases assets such as copyrights and patents that have been shown to have definite limited lives may be amortized.

Examples of intangible assets that might be amortized are goodwill and other intangibles purchased; start-up costs; organization costs; research and experimental costs; a covenant not to compete; patents; copyrights; and customer lists. Amortization expenses are added to business earnings to complete the variable: <u>EBITDA</u>. This is a more accurate indicator of the business earning power. A sample earnings reconstruction below reveals EBITDA to be 50.23% greater than business net profit.

EARNINGS RECONSTRUCTION Bell-Quest, ltd.	
Revenue	$608,951
Cost of Goods	<$397,530>
Gross Profit	$211,421
Expenses	<$189,501>
Net Profit	$ 21,920
Interest	$ 4,533
Taxes	-----
EBIT	$ 26,453
Depreciation	$ 4,809
Amortization	$ 1,668
EBITDA	$ 32,930

Cash Flow

Although depreciation and amortization are two widely accepted additions to business earnings, there are others. These can be related to the purpose of a valuation that may include a significant change in management strategy or sale of the business. The valuation consultant will attempt to see beyond the transition planned and identify new expenses that do not exist under the present circumstances. Expenses could create increases or decreases in EBITDA. These adjustments, positive and negative, are added or subtracted from EBITDA to identify a business's "cash flow". Used in this more common vernacular, cash flow is very often greater. It is earnings available to ownership following the expected change in business strategy or ownership, provided the previous year's business results remain unchanged. Cash flow therefore is a critical variable.

Weighted Cash Flow

There are occasions when use of one year's cash flow increases investment risk. A weighted cash flow is helpful when a business is experiencing strong growth trends or downturns in results. This device will diminish the influence of trends on business cash flow and is used as a replacement for one year's cash flow. This approach is less aggressive but it remains reliable thereby reducing risk to the investor.

To calculate a weighted cash flow, the current year and the previous one or two years' of operating statements are used. An ERCON is performed with each year. Thereafter, a weighting scale is used. When using the current and one previous year, the current year cash flow is multiplied by two and added to the previous year. Then, divide the result three to produce a cash flow estimate weighted two-to-one in favor of the current year.

Effective Phrase

"I'm not showing anyone my books!"

Business owners who say this demonstrate their resistance to an earnings reconstruction. Ask them, "Which indicator of performance do you suppose can justify a higher value for your business - taxable net profit or cash flow?" Explained this way, owners understand the value of disclosures. In fact, some tell more than they should.

When three years' of results are used, multiply the current year's cash flow by three, the previous year's cash flow by two and add cash flow from the earliest year. Divide the combined result by six to produce a cash flow that bears a 3:2:1 weighting. Again, current trends are given greater emphasis but not used exclusively for the valuation analysis.

"Perks"
Positive Adjustments to Earnings

Perks are several types of expenses that may be added in part or entirely to earnings. Many will fall into the following categories: education, employee benefits, entertainment, home office, interest, non-recurring expenses, payroll, transportation and travel–in in addition to depreciation and amortization. The discussion that assumes deductions for certain expenses is allowed by IRC guidelines. Taxation rules and regulations are sometimes warped beyond recognition by ownership pursuing an aggressive tax avoidance strategy. They are further complicated by the frequent changes in the IRS code. Justification for certain expenses provides the basis for adjustment–addition to earnings. Conference with professional representatives of the business and, in all cases, review the current IRC rules to determine what adjustments are, and are not, allowable. Nothing provided in this text overrules the current IRS code, which is the final authority. The following is a list of generally recognized adjustments.

Education

Education expenses might be deducted provided the purpose of the education is deemed required or necessary for the pursuit of business activity. Generally, if the education is needed to improve business skills or meet legal or licensing requirements, it is deductible.

It is fairly easy to imagine a situation where a buyer with considerable experience is acquiring a business. Education expenses for employees of the previous owner may no longer be necessary; thus, these could be considered additions to earnings.

Employee Benefits

Employee benefits are paid to employees of the business who receive compensation. The most common form of employee benefit is insurance. Medical insurance is costly, and premiums paid to a departing owner may be considered cash flow if not reassigned to a new owner. The same can be said of life insurance used to fund an estate, or company contributions to a pension plan. If not to be paid to new ownership, these are adjustments to earnings.

Entertainment

Entertaining clients in the course of business is a common practice (sometimes more necessary than desired). Ownership entertaining itself is not the same, however. A portion of entertainment expenses may be deductible according to current IRC rules if they are considered directly related or associated with business activity.

Abuses occur when the entertainment is less related to business and more related to personal enjoyment. The deductibility of entertainment expenses is subject to strict rules. Generally, 50% of entertainment and meal expenses are not allowed for deductions provided they are not considered excessive. If it is suggested that entertainment expenses are greater than necessary, that portion not required may be added to earnings.

Home Office

The most rapidly growing form of business deduction involves use of a home office. This is a result of the rapid expansion of telecommuting opportunities and the formation of home-based businesses. The Taxpayers Relief Act of 1997 (TRA 1997) provides that business deductions for home expenditures can be made if the office 1) Is used as a principal place of business for the business activity, 2) Is used as a location to meet clients or customers during the normal course of business or 3) Is located in a structure not attached to the home but at the same location.

Deductions made are those that relate directly or indirectly to the office. This covers basic operating expenses, decorating and a prorated share of expenses that benefit the entire home. These would be mortgage interest or rent, real estate taxes, insurance, utilities and maintenance.

When a home-based business is to be acquired and moved, it is evident the home office business expenses will be discontinued. If the current owner makes deductions for the home office, they may be treated as adjustments to earnings. They will be discontinued under new ownership and cease to exist.

Interest

Mortgage interest costs are usually removed as a cost of doing business when performing an ERCON. This is because valuation formulas begin with cash flow as a key valuation variable. Committing a large portion cash flow to the payment of a large mortgage may affect business equity. Value however is the combination of equity and debt. Since most valuations are performed to serve an acquisition objective, new financing is often contemplated. Therefore, interest costs related to existing financing on a business frequently changes. Existing mortgage expenses are often treated as positive adjustments to earnings.

An exception with interest can occur when financing is needed to support normal business operations. This frequently happens when inventory is financed and there is no plan to own this asset outright. Interest costs related to maintenance of an inventory would not be added to earnings provided there is no change of strategy to eliminate them altogether.

Another occasion will exist when the business has wide variances in selling cycles creating the need for large cash reserves. Unless operations are funded from ownership equity (cash), interest tied to a line of credit will occur. These are not added as adjustments to earnings.

Non-recurring Expenses

There may be instances when expenses have been incurred but will not be repeated. This occurs with expenses that may be expensed rather than depreciated or amortized over time. Typical examples of non-recurring expenses are certain types of repairs and maintenance, an increase in the business inventory, addition of small equipment and so forth. If it is recognized that these costs were unique and will occur only once, they may become adjustments to earnings.

Payroll

It is common for owners of a business to pay themselves a salary. This will normally be found in the salaries or general payroll expense. It may also be placed in the officers' salaries when the business is a corporation.

In general, payroll and officers' salaries may be considered adjustments to earnings when one of the following two conditions exists. First, payment is made from either expense to compensate a departing operating owner *who can be adequately replaced by a new operating owner.* They will acquire the existing owner's payroll and/or officer's salary. Second are payments to compensate individuals who do not perform services for the company. Sometimes this occurs with board members or a CEO advisory board. They are compensated from officers' salaries in exchange for their participation at quarterly board meetings. If deemed unnecessary by new ownership, this expense may be treated as an adjustment to earnings.

In some cases, only a portion of the compensation to an existing owner will be recaptured as earnings. One example occurs when a new owner feels the owner's existing compensation should be split between themselves and some other type of new expense–perhaps an additional employee. Another occasion arises when a new owner elects to commit a portion of the current owner's compensation to payment of financing created to acquire the business. (This is discussed in greater detail within subsequent chapters.)

On occasion a new owner will reduce the staff of a business. This can occur if existing management has been in place for many years, has become complacent or tends to favor certain employees despite their level of performance. Eliminating jobs or people is an unpleasant as well as risky management tactic for a new owner. On the surface it does not capture the trust or loyalty of remaining employees either. Cutbacks can, however, be very timely and appropriate, plus produce a desired result–improved earnings. When this is the case, firm, decisive management is rewarded with improved earnings. This will reestablish the confidence, pride and support needed from company employees.

Conversely, no adjustment to earnings occurs when new management does not plan to replace existing management and assume their wages. This occurs occasionally when entrepreneurs target a business for addition to their portfolio and encourage existing management to continue. Or, they may hire new management altogether. Wages paid to existing management are not earnings adjustments.

Transportation

Transportation costs deducted are taxi fares, train fares, airline tickets, and so forth. These are deductible when they occur in the course of travel for business purposes. Most common of the transportation expenses is the automobile and truck expense, which frequently appears in the business operating statement. Methods of determining the auto expense taken will vary. The bigger question pertains to the use of the vehicle for business or personal purposes. Answering this question will determine the availability of adjustment if warranted.

Travel

Generally speaking, travel expenses are deductible if the owner traveled to engage in trade or business activity. Travel expenses include transportation, meals, lodging and other reasonable and necessary expenses while "away from home." The IRS takes the position that to qualify, the person traveling must be away from home overnight or for a period of time that will require some rest before returning home. Many business owners will participate in business and personal activities when traveling. The question of deductibility often occurs. The prevailing determinant is whether the travel was business or personal. There are many other rules that govern the deductibility of travel expenses that can be found in IRC rules. In any event, some travel costs appearing in business expenses may be personal or entirely unnecessary in the future. Therefore, a positive adjustment is calculated as the extent to travel costs are reduced. It is added to earnings.

The amount of adjusting estimated to occur is limited only by entrepreneurial creativity. These will always be found in the expenses of the business. Draws to ownership appearing in the balance sheet are not positive adjustments. Suspicious increases in cost of goods inferring owner's use of personal merchandise are not positive adjustments. Skimming is not. Nevertheless, when all are considered, these adjustments are capable of producing dramatic changes in the business earning power recognized. This will directly affect business value.

"Plows"
Negative Adjustments to Earnings

Negative adjustments earn the nickname "Plows" because they dig into and reduce business EBIT, EBITDA and cash flow. These are expenses the business does not have prior to a transition but will incur afterward. They are not particularly common, but it is always wise to try and detect their presence.

There are many examples of negative adjustments. The most obvious is an increase in leased payments or rent occurring as a condition of a business transfer. Recent property assessments may create a rise in business or real property taxes. The husband and wife team departing as operating owners may create a need for another employee. New marketing to expand business share could be necessary. Deferred maintenance or new equipment purchases for expansion are another.

To identify negative adjustments, discuss current operations with ownership. What improvements to the business are desirable—which are required? The latter, together with any other negative adjustments, should be subtracted from cash flow.

Cash Flow Calculation

CASH FLOW CALCULATIONS BELL-Quest, Ltd.	
Revenue	$608,951
Cost of Goods	<$397,530>
Gross Profit	$211,421
Expenses	<$189,501>
Net Profit	$ 21,920
Interest	$ 4,533
Taxes	-----
EBIT	$ 26,453
Depreciation	$ 4,809
Amortization	$ 1,668
EBITDA	$ 32,930
Non-Recurring Expenses	$502
Owner's Salary	$18,000
CASH FLOW	$ 51,432

The completed ERCON presents a very clear estimate of the business's earning power. As previously stated, this is the business cash flow. This number may be a derivative of the most current business operating statement, or a weighted average of the past three.

One Business – Many Values

As an ERCON is performed, the buyer begins to see why a business can have many different values. Adjustments to earnings available to one investor may not be suitable for another. A situation involving any of those adjustments previously discussed could be found to apply. As a result, the cash flow available will bear a corresponding difference. The chapters explaining valuation techniques will illustrate how cash flow affects value, too. More cash flow tends to produce a higher value, and the reverse is also true.

Here, then, is a quantifiable reason one business could be worth more than one value. It depends on the needs of an interested investor. Those who can extract the most cash flow realize more benefits and can justify a larger investment.

In the end, the valuation consultant does not attempt to build a one-size-fits-all value estimate. The better approach is to define a value range. Where a business sale is anticipated, the reconstruction and value estimate is designed to meet the needs of most buyers in the largest target market. Business valuation becomes a powerful marketing tool.

6

Management Compensation
Perk or Plow?

**"Good judgment comes from experience.
Experience comes from bad judgment."**

It is common for the same person to wear the hat of owner and manager in a small business, receiving the dual benefits available to ownership and management. This can be a significant benefit of small business ownership. Attempting to wear both hats simultaneously, however, is a more challenging proposition. For example, both a cowboy hat and baseball cap shelter the sun from the wearer's eyes. They perform similar if not identical functions. Yet attempting to wear them both at the same time actually reduces rather than improves the benefit of each. They may both fit the same head – but not necessarily at the same time.

The story about hats is a helpful metaphor that applies to business ownership and management. The cash flow of many small business operations may be insufficient to pay management compensation at "market rates" plus generate a handsome return to ownership. This does not, however, diminish interest in small business ownership for the purpose of creating an employment opportunity for oneself. People want to buy a job. In fact, the same people that own small businesses usually run them, too. The danger lies in attempting to fill the roles of ownership and management simultaneously. It takes focus to execute the responsibilities of both positions efficiently. Distractions, reducing focus, are the frequent result of acting both as manager and owner. This can lead to poor financial results – a primary cause of business failure.

Establishing a Pay Rate

The leveraged cash flow methods of business valuation require management costs to be considered before a value is determined. Therefore, it is necessary to determine accurate management costs prior to calculating business value. This is an important valuation variable. As discussed, this should be considered separately from a return on ownership's investment, *even though the owner and manager might be the same person.*

Several approaches to assign management compensation are available to the valuation analyst. The current ownership compensation package is always a good example to consider. Be aware, however, that many times the employment earnings of owner/operators will have become inconsistent with the local market. They own the place and can pay themselves as much or as little as they like. In some cases the salary will be small and supplemented with business profits. In others the salary is large compared to compensation for similar jobs in other businesses. It is wise to be careful when using existing management compensation (to an operating owner) as a benchmark to estimate the future cost of business supervision.

An alternative way to determine management compensation involves going directly to the market. Research wages other companies offer to those who would fill supervisory roles similar in skill requirements, responsibility and authority. Newspaper classified ads, industry trade journals, local accountants, lenders and competitors are good sources of accurate information. Analysts have been known to conduct surveys as a device to encourage participation and legitimate input. The results of the survey are distributed to contributors who receive the benefit of this valuable market information.

The U.S. Government provides a third source of data entrepreneurs can use to determine management compensation. One document available and of particular interest is called "Household Data Annual Averages." This material describes the results of a nationwide survey of compensation amounts for hundreds of employment positions. The data shows occupation, year of survey, number of workers included in the survey, and median weekly earnings for each worker. It also indicates earning variances between men and women.

Internet Reference

Bureau of Labor Statistics
http://www.bls.gov

The Bureau of Labor Statistics is the principal fact-finding agency for the Federal Government in the broad field of labor economics and statistics. The BLS conducts a Current Population Survey (CPS) to measure the extent of unemployment in the country. The CPS has been conducted in the United States every month since 1940. Included in this report are Labor Force Statistics, including weekly earnings data.

The Household Data report provides a rich source of current information for the business valuation consultant. This changes and is updated annually. To use this report correctly, identify one or more positions that match or are similar to the management position in the business under study. Working with one of these median weekly earnings values (or the average of several), multiply the weekly earnings by 52 (the number of weeks in the year) to estimate annual management costs. It is that simple, however, it is wise to challenge this estimate by comparing it to local pay levels. Thereafter, make any adjustments felt necessary in order to account for geographic or economic variances. The tables and current data on file with the United States Bureau of Labor Statistics can be found online at their website.

For the example in this text the tables from 2000 are used. It is assumed the business is a sales-oriented enterprise. From the job classification "Supervisors," in the Proprietors/Sales Occupations, the average median weekly income is $608. This is $31,616 per year (averaged to $31,500) and will be used to estimate an important business valuation variable - free cash flow.

Free Cash Flow

The rewards of ownership and employment (management) become as different as the contribution required to create them. Think of it: by providing capital and financing an entrepreneur can own a business without operating it. Conversely, a manager can apply experience, skill and time to manage a business successfully but not own it. One is concerned directly with business value – the other indirectly. Therefore, to calculate business value the analyst must separate the costs of management · from financial rewards of ownership, as explained previously. Then business value is a derivative of earning power, assuming all the pieces and parts to deliver the return on investment are firmly in place. Leaving anything out results in an overestimation of value. The remaining funds, representing the financial reward to ownership, are free cash flow. Like its compensation counterpart, this will be used extensively in the valuation estimates.

Calculating free cash flow is easy. Cash flow is determined by performing an ERCON. When completed, the cost of management compensation is subtracted from cash flow. Free cash flow is the remainder. Examine the formula to determine this variable:

CASH FLOW CALCULATION BELL-Quest, Ltd.	
Revenue	$ 608,951
Cost of Goods	<397,530>
Gross Profit	211,421
Expenses	<189,501>
Net Profit	$ 21,920
Interest	4,533
Taxes	0.00
EBIT	$ 26,453
Depreciation	4,809
Amortization	1,668
EBITDA	32,930
Non-Recurring Expenses	502
Owner's Salary	18,000
CASH FLOW	$ 51,432
Management Compensation	<$ 31,500>
FREE CASH FLOW	$ 19,932

Better Safe Than Sorry

As variables for valuation are developed, they become standards to define realistic investment expectations for management and ownership.

Try to remain neutral and objectively interpret data intrinsic and extrinsic [the numbers and the marketplace] to the business under review. Balance the excitement of buying or selling against marketplace variables that can be backed up (to the extent possible) with facts. A value calculated in these conditions will often meet the needs of all parties to a transaction. Buyers will not go broke attempting to make a deal that simply costs too much: sellers will not languish in the market until it's time to give up and liquidate for half the original business value.

7

Using Other People's Money to Buy a Business

"How you pay for a business is as important as how much you pay."

A business, not a home, may be the largest investment an entrepreneur will make, however, the amount of cash needed to buy a business "outright" is often more than most have available. Fortunately, it is possible to start small and grow. But financing, using other people's money, makes it possible to start a little bigger and grow a little faster. Employing this strategy over several years has great potential. Consider the following scenario.

Once a business is acquired growing can require cash - too often more than is produced from business earnings. Financing plays an important role at this stage by ensuring growth plans can be implemented.

When it is time to sell out, sellers typically want as much cash as they can get. In most cases, this is only possible by working to accommodate the needs of a buyer – who may need to borrow a portion of the business purchase price.

In each instance, financing from others provides entrepreneurs with the leverage often needed to build greater wealth. Financing involves several basic elements. Learning these enables financing to be structured advantageously. As a consequence, the price and terms both count.

Suppose an entrepreneur acquires a small business worth $100,000 using a $25,000 down payment and finances the balance for five years. Business cash flows retire the debt during that time and the business appreciates at a modest rate of one percent annually. After the fifth year of ownership, the business is sold. Estimate 70 percent of the sales price (after taxes) is reinvested as a 25 percent down payment on another business purchased under the same conditions. This cycle is repeated four times in 20 years with the following results.

25%Initial Investment	New Business Price	Sales Proceeds Before Taxes	Cash to Pocket or Reinvest
$25,000	$100,000	$105,101	$73,571
$73,571	$294,283	$309,294	$216,506
$216,506	$866,024	$910,200	$637,140
$637,140	$2,548,559	$2,678,561	$1,874,993

Close to $2 Million of equity is created after 20 years from an average annual return of 21.78%. This does not include compensation received and accumulated savings along the way.

Capitalization Rates

The term capitalization rate refers to the rate at which a stream of future payments converts into a present value. The concept is also called the "cap rate" or simply "CAP." In any case it is expressed as a rate, like interest. For example, an investment capable of producing $1,000 of income capitalized at 10% indicates a present value of $10,000. As the cap rate declines, the value of the investment increases: conversely, increasing it reduces the size of investment indicated. Consider the following examples showing the impact of a 3% variance in the capitalization rate.

$1,000 (income) ÷ 10% (cap) = $10,000 (value)

$1,000 (income) ÷ 8.5% (cap) = $11,764.70 (value)

$1,000 (income) ÷ 11.5% (cap) = $8,695.65 (value)

Investors who expect lower prices and greater value select higher cap rates. Buyers use higher cap rates that indicate lower investment requirements. Investors and ownership both use a capitalization rate to measure the current performance of a business. It can help set expectations of performance, such as, "The business plan for next year offers ownership a 7% rate of return on assets." Or it can be used to value a business when introduced with income into a valuation formula.

Notice how the capitalization formula could be used to incorporate business income (I), value (V), and a rate of return (R) expected. The latter is the capitalization rate.

Selecting a Cap Rate

There are many ways to choose a capitalization rate for investment and valuation, and it is a very important decision. The cap rate is used repeatedly to compare all business investments under consideration. Investors who focus on small publicly traded companies often establish a capitalization rate as the prime lending rate plus 12 percentage points. Using this approach with a current prime rate of 8.75%, the applicable capitalization rate is 20.75%. When the earnings per share of stock are divided by this amount, the value they will pay is indicated.

Venture capitalists invest in small businesses. They typically do not want to involve themselves with management, however, and are only concerned with ROI (return on investment). Their capitalization rate may be less, prime plus 6% or 14.75%, but their package of support comes with other benefits. Generally, in exchange for providing growth capital, they have options to acquire ownership for a very favorable price. Their investment horizon is five to seven years, at which time they like to sell their interest to the original ownership. The price paid will be based on the increased value of the company. In the event management is successful, the investment is lucrative. If, however, management fails to meet well-defined performance objectives, the venture capitalists can take control of the board – thus control of the company – and sell it to recover their original investment.

Angel capital investors work like venture capitalists but typically may be less aggressive. Their formulas differ to the extent that their target business investments and commitments of capital are often smaller. They frequently provide management with consulting assistance as well, which helps to ensure the company stays on track (since the original ownership is also serving as management and the potential for distractions is high). Angel capital investors are not, however, given the sweet name because they are more generous. They typically expect investment terms and capitalization rates on par with their venture capital cousins.

American Bankers Association
www.aba.com
Based in Washington, D.C., the American Bankers Association represents banks of all sizes on issues of national importance for financial institutions and their customers.

Federal Deposit Insurance Corporation
www.fdic.gov
The Federal Deposit Insurance Corporation's mission is to maintain the stability of and public confidence in the nation's financial system.

Commercial banks are the most frequent users of capitalization rates. They have the closest and most frequent association with the small business sector. They invest money in these entities in the form of loans for acquisition and expansion. The interest rate charged on money loaned is the bank's return on investment.

A bank's capitalization rate is derived from its cost of money and cost of doing business. Combined they produce what is known as the prime rate of interest – the rate charged to the bank's customers. Small business borrowers often pay the bank a few percentage points of interest over the prime lending rate, so that is the bank's capitalization rate. This can be a good benchmark for entrepreneurs to use when selecting a capitalization rate for business investing.

Using a Cap Rate In Valuations

Use of capitalization rates when valuing a business is helpful but of limited value. They seldom take into consideration the differences between EBIT, EBITDA and business cash flow. In addition, they fail to account for the effects of financing on earnings. It takes money to pay off debt, and that money should come from business cash flow. Consequently value is often indicated using the premise that debt does not exist, which is seldom true (most businesses are acquired or expanded by securing additional financing to pay the cost). The costs of servicing debt will reduce free cash flow. Actually, in some cases it will be nearly eliminated, as free cash flow is redirected from the entrepreneur to the bank. Paying off a loan instead of paying a return to investors can be a lucrative business strategy, however. Additional benefits can be created by amortization of debt.

Financial Leverage

Some entrepreneurs believe nirvana is a no-money-down business acquisition. (This can be true.) Others feel the best situation is business ownership with no debt. After years of paying off a bank loan, the lure of debt-free status is very appealing. While not a mistake, a capital structure free of debt does not always maximize the earning potential of a business. Under the right conditions, financing might enhance a return on investment equity.

Leverage in business ownership is a way to acquire a business *without increasing ownership's investment* or equity. In fact, these are often reduced when investment leverage is used. Create investment leverage by borrowing more of the acquisition price. Or add debt to the capital structure of a business. Either way less ownership equity is invested.

Can the use of financial leverage be taken too far? Absolutely - LBO's, leveraged buyouts, are good examples. Investors using this strategy are so aggressive they attempt to finance entire purchase prices using no equity. This is a high-risk business strategy because the margin for error is small.

It will be shown in future sections describing leveraged cash flow methods of valuation how leveraged buy-outs can be structured. For the moment, remember consistent cash flows combined with favorable earnings trends are prerequisites to highly leveraged acquisitions. This is because servicing debt can require most if not all the free cash flow available. Should earnings decline, owners are faced with the unhappy proposition of supporting business debt from personal reserves.

Despite the caution, leveraging a business responsibly remains a moneymaking tool for entrepreneurs. To improve success, there are certain aspects of financing to understand and use with versatility: debt coverage ratio, loan-to-value ratio, and amortization. A discussion of each follows.

Debt Coverage Ratio

Lenders use two basic devices to limit their exposure to loss from small business loans. One limit, a debt coverage ratio, is based on business free cash flow. (The other, a loan-to-value ratio, is based on collateral and will be discussed later.)

A debt coverage ratio (DCR) is used to discount the amount of free cash flow that can be applied to payment of debt requested. This safeguard is intended to ensure that enough cash remains available to service debt even if earnings decrease. Used in this way, the DCR is a barometer reflecting the perceived risk associated with the business cash flow of the borrower.

Usually DCR and risk move up or down in relationship to each other. (The only exception is if DCR falls below 1.00 which, as a practical matter, does not occur.) There are few standards established for lenders to measure risk and assign a DCR, however, it is not entirely arbitrary. Borrower's credit history and proven management skill, stability of business earnings, liquidity of collateral – all are important considerations. Environmental forces can also play a role, which is particularly evident when stiff competition for the borrower's business makes an appearance. Therefore, the DCR is a subjective measurement of risk.

DCR's are generally between 1.00 and 1.50. When used to discount a cash flow, the latter is divided by the former. In the BELL-Quest, Ltd. example used throughout this text, free cash flow (FCF) is $19,932. This is money that could be treated as a return on investment for the cash investor or for payment on debt, or both. For simplicity assume a 100% conversion to retire debt. Assume the lender has, based on experience, selected a debt coverage ratio of 1.10. The amount of annual debt service (ADS) that can be paid will be $18,120. This is calculated as follows:

$$\frac{\$19,932}{1.10 \text{ (DCR)}} = \$18,120 \text{ (Annual Debt Service)}$$

Examine the table below to more fully understand the potential impact of DCR on annual debt service:

FCF	$19,932	$19,932	$19,932	$19,932	$19,932
DCR	1.00	1.20	1.30	1.40	1.50
ADS	$19,932	$16,610	$15,332	$14,237	$13,288

It is easy to see the impact of DCR. One-third of the business's free cash flow is eliminated for use as annual debt service when the debt coverage ratio is high. As a result, the amount of potential investment leverage is reduced. The DCR, then, is an important chess piece in the game of financing negotiation.

Loan-to-Value Ratios

A second device lenders use to limit exposure is a loan-to-value ratio (LTV). The loan-to-value ratio ties the amount that can be borrowed to the fair market value of assets available for collateral. For example, conventional home mortgages frequently have an LTV of 80%. This means the lending institution will loan the borrower up to 80% of the fair market value of the property as determined by an appraisal. Thus, a home valued at $100,000 with an 80% LTV would qualify for an $80,000 mortgage.

Banks use LTVs to guard against loss of capital. If the borrower defaults on the loan, the collateral should be enough, when sold, to satisfy the remaining balance due. Take note: If the remaining loan balance is greater than the net proceeds collected from assets sold, the borrower is still responsible for paying the difference. For this reason, smart entrepreneurs attempt to negotiate "non-recourse" notes, which exempt them from such personal liability. In any event, commercial lenders know collection is an uncertain reality when a business defaults on a loan. The LTV helps prevent such losses if an entrepreneur is forced to fold.

Loan-to-value ratios are important to consider when exploring the financing option of a small business. Like their companion, DCR, they reduce the amount of leverage available to make an acquisition. It is important to be familiar with use of LTVs. They will apply to almost every business loan made by institutional lenders and connote another chess piece to move.

There are several categories of business assets that may be used as collateral for a business loan. Real estate, furnishings/fixtures/equipment, inventory and intellectual capital all have a different lifespan. Their liquidity varies, too. Applying a 100% LTV would be almost unheard of. It is more reasonable to expect LTVs for these asset classes to fall within a range roughly described as follows:

Real Estate	75% to 90%
Furnishings/Fixtures/Equipment	50% to 75%
Inventory	25% to 50%
Intellectual Capital	0% to 25%

These are estimated ranges only and may vary from lender to lender, locale to locale and business to business. Also, keep in mind banks will seldom (if ever) offer financing using intellectual capital as collateral.

Amortization

Amortization was described earlier as an accounting charge to income based on the periodic reduction of an intangible asset's original value. A second definition is the payoff of debt through regularly timed payments of principal and interest. Payments to principal represent equal increases in equity if business value remains constant. Payments to interest are treated as deductible expenses.

Amortization of debt is useful to business valuation. After a DCR and LTV have been selected, it is possible to estimate the amount of debt a business can borrow. Calculating the amortization of the debt helps entrepreneurs create ways a business can afford the financing available. This will become evident in the leveraged cash flow method of valuation. Using amortization as a financing tool emphasizes the entrepreneur's ability to anticipate DCRs and LTVs, as well as calculate loan terms, interest rates, present value, future value and periodic payments on debt projected. This is the structure of financing and has a direct bearing on the benefits financial leverage is intended to create.

Using Financial Calculators

Inexpensive financial calculators help the valuation analyst work very fast. These devices have loan amortizing functions that vastly simplify the calculation of payments on debt. These instruments break the amortization calculation into five variables: term, interest, payment, present value and future value. With these calculators it is possible to enter any four variables and easily solve for the fifth. Here are the variables involved.

√ **Term** - Term refers to the length of time that will pass from the origination of the loan to the payoff date. There is a general rule to follow when estimating loan terms: Don't make long-term loans on short-term assets. Otherwise, the loan will remain unpaid long after the collateral asset has experienced functional or economic obsolescence or both. The lender's risk will be unacceptable.

The term of a loan should be less than and no more than the useful life of the asset. Here is a general list of loan terms to use with business assets often financed, subject to regional and individual variances:

Real Estate	15 to 30 years
Furnishings/Fixtures/Equipment	3 to 7 years
Inventory	I/O - 0 to 3 Years
Intellectual Capital	N/A

√ **I/O** - stands for interest only. Sometimes banks will finance an inventory using a line of credit loan. In these cases the borrower may pay interest only on the balance financed followed by periodic reductions in principal. There is no term. Since banks seldom loan on intellectual capital, no term is stated.

When entering the term of a loan into a financial calculator, it may be requested as *n,* which stands for the number of payments that will be made throughout the term. If monthly payments are called for, *n* is the term of the loan in years times twelve.

√ **Interest** - Interest is the cost of using money that is expressed as a rate for a period of time. The period is typically annual. As mentioned earlier, monthly payments will include interest and principal. These are calculated roughly as the interest due on the outstanding balance of the loan for the previous or coming month plus principal. The principal is the difference between the payment amount and the interest payment.

It is easy to see the interest portion of payments that occur early in the loan term will be larger than those occurring late in the loan life. This is why the same payment schedule will retire less debt early and more debt later. Many investors counteract this slow reduction of loan principal with a simple technique – by making the current payment plus the small principal payment that would be due with next month's installment as they advance their amortization schedule one month. When this occurs, the interest that would have been paid is cancelled, too. Executed consistently this provides a substantial savings of interest and reduces the loan term by 50%.

For more information about how interest rates are determined, see "Capitalization Rates" earlier in this chapter. Banks normally charge small business borrowers

1% to 3% over their prime-lending rate. Interest is either fixed or variable. If fixed, it will remain constant for a specified portion (if not the entire term) of the loan; if variable it can change periodically based on preset limits (i.e. a change of no more than 1% increase or decrease per period with a maximum cap of not more than 5% over the life of the loan). A debt with a flexible rate such as this is called an adjustable rate mortgage, or ARM.

√ **Present Value** - The present value of the loan is the amount borrowed. It is determined from the borrower's need or request when adjusted by the LTV, DCR, interest rate and term. A capitalization rate is used to measure the present value of a stream of payments to be collected in the future.

√ **Future Value** - The future value of a loan amortization is the amount of principal outstanding on the payoff date of the loan. At that time the loan balance will be zero if a loan is "fully amortized." This means the payments are enough to pay off the entire loan during the term.

In some cases, where cash flow considerations are a greater priority, equal monthly payments may not be sufficient to pay off the entire loan by the end of the loan term. An outstanding balance will be due, called a "balloon payment." In the world of finance it is common to receive a loan with an amortization term where the actual payoff of the loan from monthly payments would not occur until long after the payoff date. Loans are frequently amortized for 15 years but due in five. In this case the term of the loan is five years.

√ **Payment** - The fifth variable in the amortizing equation is the amount of money needed each period to reduce the principal and pay the interest due as agreed based on the loan term and amount. Payments may occur monthly, quarterly, semi-annually or annually. They may be amortizing or include a fixed amount of principal each month plus interest on the outstanding balance.

8 | A Pricing Multiple that Works With Any Business

"One size does not fit all."

Business RPM Calculator

A risk/price multiple (RPM) is often called a "pricing multiple." Multiples are popular yardsticks used to quickly determine a business's value. The RPM variety measures the risk and value. Used in this way it helps compare acquisition candidates. One can quickly measure the value from the risk that is indicated.

The excess earnings method of business valuation utilizes a risk/price multiple. It can also function as a guide to management since it will illustrate a business's weaknesses and strengths. It also can be used to help determine management compensation bonuses.

Risk/price multiples are more commonly used, however, as quick estimates of business value because they are so simple. For example, a business with a higher multiple is perceived as a better business than one with a lower multiple. This means the risk is less, so the value is more.

The risk/price multiple appears in many valuation rules of thumb, too. These are stated as "five times earnings" or "one and a half times revenue" and so forth. Formulas using an RPM can be quick and helpful indicators of value if developed from sound premises. Unfortunately this is not always the case.

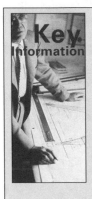

Consider a most common multiple– "five times earnings." Business owners ready to sell out often dream of notoriously high multiples. Values indicated may not offer investors enough cash flow to compensate management, provide a return on investment or service acquisition debt. The price indicated can be so high it is laughable. Buyers work in reverse – they prefer a multiple so low it would be possible to finance 150% of an acquisition price from free cash flow. The business is probably worth more than their highly leveraged estimate of value.

To further confuse the use of multiples, no clear definition is often given to the type of earnings used with the multiple. Is it net profit, EBIT, EBITDA, cash flow or free cash flow? Clearly, net profit and free cash flow will produce very different values using the same RPM. One must also question selection of the variable "5." Is it a function of the owners' desire to sell for more than the business is worth, the buyers' interest in paying less than they should, or comparative market criteria? The last option sounds most credible but only if RPM's used are developed from an accurate set of "comps." There is a better way.

Work from the Inside *and* Outside

Consider building an RPM using intrinsic business elements in addition to these other methods. Comparative data, seller expectations and buyer demands are balanced with business indicators of performance as predictors of value. These may limit the RPM's ability to produce a reliable result. Developing a risk/price multiple from external *and internal* characteristics is a better way. It takes more time and investigation, but the tool created is useful and meaningful enough to more than justify the effort.

Many Kinds of Risk to Measure

Risk in business is the possibility of losing value or failing to increase value. There are many kinds of risk: appreciation risk, inflation risk, interest rate risk, inventory risk, liquidity risk, political risk, repayment risk or risk to principal.

While all types of risk are important to small business entrepreneurs, appreciation, inventory, liquidity, repayment and risk to principal are of greatest concern.

Appreciation risk pertains to the ability of the business to grow in value. There are many reasons this can occur. Some are beyond the control of ownership, others are not. Recall, amortization applies responsible financial leverage to produce a gradual increase in ownership equity. This occurs as debt is reduced, although the potential gain available, though desirable, remains finite. Appreciation, on the other hand, offers infinite potential for increases in business value. Effective management of financial leverage, combined with gradual appreciation, has the potential to create impressive wealth over time. It also reduces the risk to principal.

> "Rule #1: Never run out of cash.
> Rule #2: Never, ever, run out of cash."
>
> *Professor Fran Jabara*

Liquidity risk is created by the possibility the business will run out of cash. The reason is, quite simply, when a business is out of cash, it is out of options. When options to carry on are removed, the business can easily fail.

Inventory risk is capturing increased attention. Dell Computer enjoys a commanding lead in the computer manufacturing industry due, in part, to their successful system of inventory management. With sales of millions per day, they have only a short-term supply of inventory on hand. Dramatic levels of functional and economic obsolescence constantly occurring in the hardware industry create great risk. Millions of dollars invested in stagnant inventory does not enhance business performance. Dell's unique approach to inventory management reduces this risk considerably.

Objectivity Would Be Nice ...

Unfortunately, there are so many different types and sizes of small businesses that a one-size-fits-all business multiple, even for specific industries, is hard to develop. That is the state of the small business environment. Multiples do remain helpful, though, and can be created from objective information.

As indicated, several factors affect development of a useful risk/price multiple. It is not possible to produce a perfect indicator of performance. The process is subjective: It's determined by the perceptions of the person conducting the analysis. With good material from a complete due diligence, the analyst can develop an RPM that is highly defensible.

To calculate a risk/price multiple, the following approach is recommended. Separate the business into six or seven categories: finance, control, marketing, sales, production, service and intellectual capital. Notice they correspond to those recommended in a due diligence investigation.

Each category is assigned a value from 0 to 5. Category values are the average of five subcategories representing characteristics of that category. These subcategories also receive a value from 0 to 5. With both categories and subcategories, high numbers indicate better quality and less risk, whereas lower numbers mean low quality and greater risk. When selecting values for each category or subcategory, it may be helpful to use the following scale for easy reference:

SCALE OF VALUES TO MEASURE BUSINESS RPM		
0	MAXIMUM RISK	Business out of control. Failure is likely.
1	HIGH RISK	Loss of equity likely. Crisis management prevails.
2	RISKY	Small margins for error, but recovery is possible.
3	ACCEPTABLE RISK.	Market and management forces can prevail.
4	LOW RISK	Good control over growth and equity. Secure.
5	MINIMAL RISK	Excellent control, many opportunities, and profitable.

The category values are averaged, and the result is the business risk/price multiple – its RPM – and an indicator of value derived from factors internal and forces external to the business.

The long-form RPM calculator can be found in the Appendix Section. Here is the short form:

BUSINESS RPM BELL-Quest, Ltd.		
1	Finance	3.0
2	Control	3.0
3	Marketing	1.0
4	Sales	2.0
5	Production	4.0
6	Service	4.0
7	Intellectual Capital	1.0
	Total	18.0
	Variables	÷7
	Business RPM	2.57

Putting It All Together

The subcategories suggested for use in calculating a business RPM may vary. Investor interests, business types and market conditions can cause this to occur. Flexibility is an important component of business valuation. Entrepreneurs building business risk/price multiples may elect to make substitutions to better suit their need.

In addition, the work to create a business RPM can become as detailed as one chooses to make it. Clearly, to develop precise information about each subcategory might require extensive investigation. Values assigned, however, remain a subjective interpretation of the entrepreneur or valuation analyst. So while investigation is a healthy exercise, one can reach a point of diminishing return.

By all means, perform a complete due diligence. Or make the due diligence as complete as time and resources permit. Then step away, adopt a fresh perspective and quickly evaluate or score each subcategory. Recalculate the business RPM. As before, first impressions based on good data most often prove correct.

Suggested RPM Categories and Subcategories

Here, together with thoughts to consider and questions to ask, are the categories and subcategories used to develop the risk/price multiple.

Finance

√ **Trailing Revenue** - Emphasis is on historical trends. Is revenue increasing each year, holding steady or declining? Normally, steadily increasing revenues are signs of a well-run business. In this case, risk would be low so the value selected would be greater. Risk is low, so the multiple is high.

Declining revenue is usually an indication of less demand for the business output of goods and services. It could also be related to limited production capability. This deserves careful study, however, declining revenue is always a strong indicator of greater business risk. Do not automatically consider rapid increases in revenue as favorable developments. Growth is the hardest part of a business to manage. Growth requires increases in capital spending to support production. If demand suddenly stops after significant investments in infrastructure have been made, cash reserves may run dry. Risk is increased.

√ **Revenue Momentum** - Significant annual improvements in business revenue are generally extrapolated into continuing increases called momentum. Determining how much momentum, translated as increased revenue, will occur next year and the year after is more difficult. This involves forecasting, which is challenging and uncertain. Unlike risk, uncertainty cannot be adequately measured.

History remains the best predictor of the future. Provided the forces that feed increases in trailing revenues remain viable, one might extrapolate continuing changes of the same, greater or lesser degree. Companies with higher momentum supported by premises expected to remain in place have less risk and a higher value. Companies with no momentum or reverse momentum have a high risk and are assigned a low value.

√ **Capital Structure** - How financially fit is the business? To determine a value for this subcategory, examine business debt and equity. When debt is more than double equity (using market value of assets), the business is highly leveraged. Risk is greater. Conversely, a business with no debt may not be risk free. It may have a lower ROI. A capital structure can also be a sign of management complacency. The business could be missing marketing opportunities repeatedly. If the business is not keeping pace, a growth wall may have been built or may be under construction. The business may not be able to handle debt. Risk could be greater. Look closely.

√ **Leverage Opportunities** - Remember, one tactic to increase return occurs with financial leverage. Businesses with no debt, as just described, may not enjoy the opportunity to create financial leverage. Since risk is greater return is lower. More importantly, financial leverage may be required to keep pace with the market. If it is not affordable, risk is greater. Businesses that can employ financial leverage to improve ROI, or to stay ahead of competitors, enjoy less risk and a higher value.

√ **Earnings and cash flow** - Clearly, those businesses with cash flow sufficient to accomplish ownership objectives are most desirable. The presence of cash increases access to more strategies. More available strategies extend the life and profitability of a business. It can be a tougher competitor. Ample cash flows reduce risk; limited cash flow increases risk.

Control

√ **Employee turnover rates and costs** - The inability to hire and retain quality employees can put a company out of business. The rate of turnover among employees is a reflection of job fit. One wrests control of business functions from management by forcing a focus on replacing and retraining people; the other seizes control of business earnings. This is a crucial consideration in a tight labor market, which many experts say will continue for the next 10 to 15 years.

Employee turnover rates are calculated as the number of employees leaving each year, for whatever reason, as a percentage of the total people employed. The national average is high, approximately 16%, which means 16% of the people that are employed today will be gone one year from today. Most companies discover their rate is as high as 30%. Turnover reduces management control.

Employee turnover costs are also much higher than most expect. It is not uncommon for the indirect and direct costs of employee turnover to exceed an employee's annual salary.

Both employee turnover rates and costs are a threat to management's control. Examine how the business addresses the issue of job fit and environment to encourage longevity. Aggressive measures reduce risk. If no measures are in place to deal with this hidden menace, risk is greater.

√ **Employee compensation** - Nothing motivates people like having a piece of the pie. Nothing demoralizes employees faster than being treated unfairly. To resolve both, management may install a written, company-wide compensation policy. With a policy in writing, trust is improved and people will perceive management as more fair. When incentives to perform behaviors that lead to improved financial results are in place, people are rewarded with validation and money. If these are delivered in amounts that are comparable with alternative employment, the system will be productive. Risk is less.

√ **Contingency planning** - Does the business have a financial plan with a revenue and expense forecast? If so, risk is a little less. Does the business have a Plan "B" or "C" in the event Plan "A" fails to produce? It is certain at least part of the original plan won't work. Options reduce risk.

Another factor affecting control and contingency planning is management's flow of control. Ownership that supports management by committee or chain of command will be outmaneuvered and outrun by aggressive competitors. Reactions are slow and often occur when it is too late. Risk is greater.

Absence of a reaction plan also increases risk. Because business moves so fast, companies must be in position to react swiftly. Unpredictable changes occur almost daily. How well does the company react to constant unpredictability? In the fast-paced world of e-commerce a good reaction plan may be the best way to reduce risk to control. Risk would be less. In the absence of a reaction, strategic operating or financial plan, risk is higher.

√ **Network penetration** - A company that builds a product that can be used by only one person is not penetrating the network of consumers available. A company that builds a product that can be used by more than one person does a better job. A company that builds a product, such as meaningful information sent by e-mail that can be read by one million people, enjoys exciting network penetration. With greater network penetration, risk is less. With no network penetration, how can the business keep pace with businesses that have developed this resource?

√ **Potential litigation** - Every business can be subject to claims from customers and competitors. Does the business have a history of lawsuits? Is there any pending litigation? Are there any outstanding judgments? One measure of exposure to litigation is activity that draws fire. Another measure is how well a company builds a defensive shield to prevent the impact of litigation should it occur. When the record shows a history of lawsuits the risk is high. Where there are none, and counter-measures are in place, risk is less.

Marketing
√ **Well-defined marketing plan** - Does the company have a written marketing plan? The ability to follow the plan to identify core values of the company with those of its target market is the key link to sales. With no plan to define and execute marketing, risk is very high. With a well-executed plan, risk is reduced.

√ **Branded power** - A brand exists to create trust. To do that it must be memorable and recognizable. It has to be delivered frequently and consistently to produce results. On the Internet, a company's brand is its substitute for the bricks and mortar of a business. Companies that successfully brand themselves will have less risk in the future compared to those that don't.

√ **Market differentiation** - Risk to a business will increase if it cannot differentiate itself from competitors. A business must be able to tell customers why it is different and why it is better. If it cannot, there is no reason for customers to patronize one business over another. When differentiation is effective, however, risk can be reduced.

√ **Market segmentation** - One does not need to sell his or her products and services to everyone in the world to be successful – just to everyone with a need for what is offered.

Kellogg's *Grape Nuts* is a breakfast cereal that sells to just 2% of the total breakfast cereal market. That small share of the market is worth $160 million a year. Because of this effective market segmentation, *Grape Nuts* is a 100-year-old company (that doesn't even sell grapes or nuts). Companies that do not know who their target market or market segment is - and therefore fail to attract them - have greater risk.

√ **E-commerce activity** - Companies that have no plan to participate in e-commerce activity have the greatest risk. It doesn't matter if they can't deliver a hamburger in cyberspace – they can use the medium to attract customers. It is said that companies with no e-commerce function will become extinct, and soon. "To attract more customers – become more attractive."

Sales

√ **Type of service/product** - Understanding the physical characteristics of a product or service is not enough to eliminate risk. One must understand what is offered in terms of its transactional, consultative or enterprise characteristics. One is a soft drink, another is advice and the third is a partnership. Failure to recognize these differences and how they are changing create greater risk.

√ **Sales process fit** - Among the most common mistakes made in sales is the mismatch of sales technique, or process, to product type. The sales process must improve the value of the product. Otherwise, it should be eliminated entirely so the product can enjoy greater price/competitive advantages and greater sales. When a mismatch occurs, the cost of sales is too high in relation to the results received. Risk is higher.

√ **Sales incentives available** - Ross Perot is a billionaire. So was Ewing Kauffman, founder of Marion Labs. Both were salespeople whose management limited their earning capability. Both quit their jobs and started their own companies for the wide-open territory of entrepreneurship. Are the business's salespeople given incentives that treat them like employees or like entrepreneurs? The latter reduces business risk.

√ **Sales training programs** - As with advertising, when business becomes unfavorable the training budget is often cut first. This does not lead to improved results. The existence of training programs in a company reduces risk. The use of them at the right time reduces it more.

√ **Wired distribution** - The no-brainer of the 21st century is distributing services via the Internet. The gains one can make in time, flexibility and costs are worth more over the long term than the development costs. As previously stated, a close association with Internet commerce reduces risk.

Production

√ **Emphasize quality** - In the absence of quality, errors will increase. This is not a new concept; William Edwards Demming introduced it as the Demming Management Method. The premise of this method is simple: More errors result in greater production costs and lower earnings. That increases risk. What steps are taken in the flow of production and service to ensure that quality maintains high? "Quality costs when you don't have it."

√ **Innovation** - In business one is either moving forward or backward. This is because standing still permits a business to fall behind compared to others sustaining forward motion. Which directions a business moves has its genesis in the business's innovative spirit. Even the Industrial Age suggestion box is an attempt to find new ideas. Employees, who see all the problems in a business first hand, have the innovative solutions needed to remove them. In the fast-paced world of business today, how well management draws out this innovative element will affect business risk favorably or unfavorably.

√ **Capacity vs. demand** - If business has the ability to produce more than it delivers, risk to revenue is less, provided there is a growing demand for products and services produced. Companies without the capacity to meet demand are growing, but also have greater risk to their survival.

√ **Obsolescence** - Whether functional or economic, obsolescence has been shown to be a loss of asset value. Risk to principal increases in the face of obsolescence. Examine production process and equipment for obsolescence. It is a direct measure of business risk.

√ **Inventory management** - It was mentioned previously that Dell Computer Company has used sound principles of inventory management to reduce risk. Another device is access to inventory. Examine how well the business maximizes its ability to order, receive and manage inventory. Those who do it most efficiently, for the least amount of investment, have the least risk.

Service

√ **Customer satisfaction** - This is an intangible asset that money cannot buy. Good impressions on the part of customers are hard to earn. They are easy to keep as long as service is maintained. If lost, satisfaction takes years to rebuild. The analyst should take the time to interview a few customers of the business and attempt to determine their level of satisfaction. If the business is well thought of, risk is less.

√ **Employee Recognition** - Pay is not a motivator. Recognition from a peer group is more powerful. Businesses who recognize this important concept offer programs that recognize superior achievement. Employees respond with superior performance. When employees are recognized for their hard work the risk is less.

√ **Team Spirit** - Peter Drucker has said a management team is one of the most powerful new tools in the manager's toolbox. Teams assigned to specific functions have the potential to produce more results, as a unit, than the team members functioning individually. Teams help businesses reduce risk.

√ **Flexibility** - Stellar service in small businesses is often linked to flexibility. It can be their greatest strength when facing larger competitors who are often unable to quickly adapt to marketplace changes. As a result growth walls are less likely to develop in a small entrepreneurial company. Their search for new ideas is constant. When found they are quickly put to use. Flexibility and adaptability reduce risk.

√ **Open communication** - Employees, customers and associates represent a rich source of feedback. This information has the potential to offer the most valuable service improvements a company can achieve. Companies that encourage communication from all sources have less chance of losing touch with the marketplace – and less risk.

Intellectual Capital

√ **Vision** - The old adage still applies, "It is easier to cross the country with a map and a destination than by wandering aimlessly about." Without a vision of where the business is headed, uncertainty can prevail in the minds of customers, employees, investors and professional representatives. Being a winner means knowing what winning means. Everyone wants to hitch his or her wagon to a winner.

√ **Integrated vision** - Look for signs the vision is integrated into the everyday thinking of employees and customers. This improves retention and results. It is the foundation of quality service. With no vision, crisis management can prevail and risk is higher.

√ **Employee Autonomy** - Are employees given an environment where they can do whatever is necessary to produce results? Is this type of autonomy encouraged? These forces, combined with others, build employee motivation. Try to imagine a business succeeding when the employees don't care. The risk will be very high.

√ **Synergy** - This occurs when combined expenses produce a result that is greater than the two expenses treated separately. Synergy is the basis for many business mergers. Operating costs for the new entity are lower while revenues and earnings increase. Synergies are easy to find but hard to make work, however. In fact, many companies that grow by acquisition discover in the final analysis, the cost did not outweigh the benefits. Still, the presence of synergy among categories considered in the risk/price multiple can reduce risk.

√ **Key people** - Management and people are important assets in a business. Unfortunately, some expect to be treated in a manner that is disproportionate to their value. Look for redundancy in job functions; does more than one person know how to perform a critical skill? Where this exists, risk resulting from the loss of a key employee is less.

√ **Institutional intelligence** - Coca-Cola has a secret formula. Microsoft has a source code. None can argue, the value of this institutional intelligence has propelled both to roles as corporate leaders on a global scale. Institutional intelligence is an old idea that continues to thrive in a new economy. As with people, businesses can have trade secrets that represent a rich source of intellectual capital. These are patents, copyrights, production processes or consumer intelligence.   When properly leveraged these intangible assets can provide a distinctive competitive edge. That reduces risk. When all competitors are able to do the same thing, risk is greater.

9

Get Quick Answers
The Capitalization Method

"I could have used any one of several equations to calculate the theory of relativity. I only chose this one because it has the most esthetic appeal – was the most beautiful and simply elegant."

Paraphrased from Albert Einstein

The capitalization method is a market approach used to determine business value. This is not because it relies on the traditional method of using comparable sales to estimate value. It employs, instead, comparable [capitalization] rates of return that might be available from alternative investments or other business opportunities. Therefore, selecting the best capitalization rate and most appropriate form of business income are important considerations when using this technique. They will affect the valuation estimate.

The Essence of the Capitalization Method

A basic mathematical equation is used to perform this valuation technique. It is amazingly easy to do. All one needs do to perform the capitalization method accurately is select the proper variables and apply basic multiplication and division skills. A common name for the equation used to execute the capitalization method is the IRV formula. It is given this name because the equation uses three variables, which are I (income), R (rate or cap rate) and V (value). Using the business earning power (intrinsic qualities) and rates of return investors expect (extrinsic qualities) the valuation consultant can easily calculate a business value. The IRV equation is:

$$\frac{I}{R \times V}$$

Using any two of these variables it is possible to calculate the third.

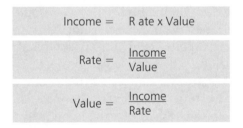

Therefore, when one knows the income produced by an investment and the market rate expected it is possible to quickly estimate the cash value of the investment. Alternatively, one who knows the rate of return expected and the value, or asking price, can estimate the income that should be available from that business. And knowing the income produced and the business value enables the valuation consultant to calculate the capitalization rate of return available.

The Benefits of Flexibility. Substituting variables, estimated versus actual, is a feature of this technique that offers impressive flexibility. It can be used to quickly pre-qualify business investments. In most instances an investor seeking to acquire a business will know the asking price and acceptable cap rates. Multiplying one by the other suggests the amount of income that should be available. A simple earnings reconstruction can be performed to determine if this is the case. If the actual income is less than estimated, the business may be overpriced. If the income is more than estimated, the business could represent a good value.

An initial calculation of value using the capitalization method allows a business buyer to quickly determine whether the asking price is too high or low. Also, it is possible to calculate a business value expected from actual income. Accomplish this by using actual income and the cap rate expected. Conversely, one could use actual income and asking price to examine the rate of return available.

It is quickly evident that this formula gives the investor a great deal of flexibility to quickly determine business value and ROI offered, based on business income.

Use the Correct Variables

Recall, success in business valuation depends on the correct selection of variables used in the formulas. The capitalization method is no exception. Follow these steps to produce the best results when using the formula.

STEP 1: Select the Correct Income

Four types of income can be used in the capitalization method: EBIT, EBITDA, cash flow, and free cash flow. In most cases of small business valuation, the income used will be free cash flow – cash flow less estimated management compensation. Review the earnings summary from the example presented earlier.

STEP 2: Select the Right Rate of Return (Cap Rate)

The earlier discussion of cap rates used in small business valuation indicated several approaches are available to set the rate. There also are several rates to consider. Interest rates can vary widely over time. To account for these variances and maintain a consistent approach throughout this text the following rates are used.

Federal lending rate	5.75%
Prime lending rate (P)	8.75%
Small business lending rate	P +<2.00% 8.75% to 10.75%
SBA lending rate	P+2.25--2.75% 11.0% to 11.5%
Safe rate (>5 year CD's)	6.00% to 6.50%

The small-business lending rate offered by commercial banks is a good starting point. There are many reasons to use it:

✓ A lender's cap rate is frequently charged by sellers electing to finance the sale of their business. Remember, the interest rate charged to the borrower is the rate of return received by the lender.

✓ It reflects local market conditions.

✓ It permits lenders to cover their operating costs and generate a profit.

104

✓ It incorporates risk of the investment; the higher the perceptions of risk, the higher the rate.

✓ The prime rate offered by banks is not affected by changes in business value. At a constant market rate, increases in business income favorably affect business value. The investor's return improves.

✓ For this illustration the cap rate selected is Prime (8.75%) plus 2.75%, or 11.5%.

STEP 3: Calculate the Value

Divide the income by the rate. This is the value of the investment indicated. Assume maximum SBA lending rates as applicable investor's capitalization rate.

$$\$19,932 \ (I) \div 11.5\% \ (R) = 173,322 \ (V)$$

From this equation a business value of $173,322 is indicated. This value, taken from trailing earnings, will provide an investor with an 11.5% return on investment after costs of compensation to management. Entrepreneurs who prefer to operate their business investments would receive management earnings in addition to their return. The combined financial benefit to an operating owner is $51,432. This is how many small business owners perceive and measure the economic reward available to ownership.

The formula for estimating business value using the Capitalization Method looks like this.

Income @ $19,932
Rate @ 11.50% = Value @ $173,322

As mentioned, the income of an investment is frequently unavailable in the early stages of an entrepreneur's discovery process. Following is an illustration of how using the equation with different variables can produce an alternative value. At a given value of $173,322 and investor expected ROI of 11.5%, income should be:

11.5% (R) x $173,322 (V) = $19,932 (I)

Substituting Variables

Suppose free cash flow is less. How will this affect the business value and rate of return? Using business income of $15,000 with no change in the asking price indicates the rate of return will be 8.65%.

$15,000 (I) ÷ $173,322 (V) = 8.65% (R)

The investor has a decision to make. Is the ROI of 8.65% still acceptable, despite its 2.85% actual variance from the market rate chosen? This is also 24.78% less than desired. Or, can the value be adjusted so the desired rate of return is preserved. To calculate the value indicated by the lower income:

$15,000 (I) ÷ 11.5% (R) = $130,435 (V)

The new value indicated is $42,887 less. AND IF CASH FLOW IS MORE adjusting the formula increases the rate available. To compensate, ownership may elect to raise the value.

$$\$25,000 \text{ (I)} \div \$173,322 \text{ (V)} = 14.42\% \text{ (R)}$$

Or

$$\$25,000 \text{ (I)} \div 11.5\% \text{ (R)} = \$217,391 \text{ (V)}$$

Use this simplest of valuation formulas to quickly determine business value. The flexibility of variable substitution permits easy calculation of alternative values and the results they can or should produce. Verify the results with valuation techniques derived from cost and income factors.

10

The Value Of Good Will
The Excess Earnings Method

**"Goodwill is generally overrated
by those who don't have it."**

The cost approach to valuing commercial real estate builds on the cost to acquire similar assets. Costs of comparable buildings or improvements, furnishings, fixtures and equipment are combined. The latter may be discounted, too, for obsolescence observed.

A second valuation technique that is easy to learn and use is the excess earnings method. It is similar to a real estate cost approach because adding costs to acquire tangible and intangible property forms the basis for value. The excess earnings method helps define what these are worth if purchased separately or if alternative businesses capable of producing the same economic result were acquired instead. This correlation to asset values differentiates the excess earnings method from other valuation techniques.

The Excess Earnings Method

Excess earnings are business free cash flow less a return on the market value, or cost, of tangible business assets. The resulting amount is inferred to be cash generated by the business goodwill or "intangibles."

The excess earnings method of business valuation is widely used. Although it works well with businesses that are asset intensive, it can also prove useful with service companies where dependence on unique people or assets is high. Obviously, it's a good approach for small businesses because it quickly separates the value of hard assets from "goodwill." The value of the latter is a pressing concern for most business owners and investors.

"What's my goodwill worth"? This is a question business owners often ask during their term of ownership. Their calculation of goodwill is often a groundless estimate plucked out of thin air with no basis in logic. Here is a response to offer regardless of the owner's estimate. "First, goodwill is only one type of a class of property known as intangible assets. Their value is calculated after business value is determined, not the other way around. The value of intangibles, including goodwill, is the difference between a business's overall value and the fair market value of its tangible assets." This leads the business owner directly into a discussion of the benefits and procedures to determine business value. That is the objective.

This method of valuation helps confirm or improve on values established by the Capitalization or Leveraged Cash Flow methods.

To calculate business value using this method, the following variables are needed:

- ✓ Free cash flow

- ✓ Market value of tangible assets

- ✓ Safe rate of return

- ✓ Business RPM

Free cash flow, market value of tangible assets and RPM are developed as described earlier. A safe rate of return is the return on investment or "interest rate" one might receive from a highly liquid short-term investment. This is often two to three points less than Prime. A good example is the rate of interest offered on a short-term certificate of deposit.

With these variables in place value may be estimated using the following steps.

STEP 1: Determine Business Free Cash Flow

This figure comes from the ERCON prepared to identify cash flow adjusted for management compensation.

Business Free Cash Flow = $19,932

STEP 2: Calculate a Return on Tangible Assets

Ask, "What could the investment in market value of tangible assets be earning if the money were invested elsewhere?" To determine this, multiply their market value by the safe rate of return.

The market (not book) value of assets includes (for purposes of a business sale), the following assets:

✓ Real Estate @ $105,000

✓ Inventory @ cost totaling $55,000

✓ Furnishings, Fixtures and Equipment @ $5,000

✓ Total $165,000

$165,000
X 6.00% (safe rate of return)
$9,900 (return on tangible assets)

STEP 3: Determine The Business Excess Earnings.

Subtract the return on investment in tangible assets (see
-Step 2) from free cash flow.

$19,932 (free cash flow)
less $9,900 (return on tangibles)
$10,032 (excess earnings)

STEP 4: Calculate Market Value of
Business Excess Earnings

This is the excess earnings multiplied by the business
RPM.

$10,032 (excess earnings)
X   2.57 (RPM)
$25,782 (excess earnings or goodwill)

STEP 5: Determine Estimated Business Value

Add the market value of business excess earnings to the
market value of business tangible assets.

$165,000 (tangibles)
+ $25,782 (value of excess earnings)
$190,782 (business value)

Applying the Excess Earnings Method

Use the excess earnings method to complement or confirm value determined by the capitalization method. As mentioned, this technique makes it easy to identify how much goodwill is worth. Notice how the formula automatically assigns a value to goodwill by identifying the income it creates. With this ability, it's easy to measure the growth of goodwill by recalculating value over time.

Key Information

Many buyers have discovered that business sellers often attempt to justify value by emphasizing how much more their business could be worth if certain initiatives were taken. A smart buyer will request predictions of investment required and income produced. Thereafter, the excess earnings valuation technique can be used to predict changes in tangible asset values and free cash flow and, from there, the "potential" business value is calculated. One quickly discovers the effort to create additional goodwill may not be as productive as envisioned. This is a good tool and technique for buyers dealing with sellers attempting to sell business potential instead of current or trailing earnings.

EXCESS EARNINGS
VALUATION METHOD
BELL-QUEST, LTD.

Variables		
Free Cash Flow		$ 19,932
Safe Rate		6%
Tangible Assets		$ 165,000
RPM		2.57
Business Free Cash Flow		$ 19,932
Tangible Assets	165,000	
Safe Rate of Return	6.00%	
Return on Tangible Assets		< 9,900>
Business Excess Earnings		$ 10,032
Risk/Price Multiple		2.57
Value of Excess Earnings		$ 25,782
Value of Tangible Assets		$ 165,000
ESTIMATED BUSINESS VALUE		$ 190,782

Like the capitalization method, the excess earnings technique is a relatively simple calculation. Accuracy and reliability is affected by variables developed and used.

11

The Gold Standard: The
Leveraged Cash Flow Method

**"A small business is often a job for sale.
A million dollar solution is not needed
for a problem of this size."**

What Buyers Want

The leveraged cash flow (LCF) method is an income approach to value. It addresses two important buyer objectives based on current market conditions: 1) paying management compensation and 2) paying off debt created to buy the business. It enables the valuation consultant to establish a value that includes debt and equity. Therefore, the leveraged cash flow method offers a value and a transaction structure. This practical approach is the gold standard of business valuation.

The leveraged cash flow method is useful because many interested in buying a business are really replacing employment by another with self-employment. These buyers do not always view a business acquisition dispassionately – their emphasis is on replacing income and not necessarily creating a return on investment. In addition, most small businesses that sell often involve some type of acquisition financing. Leverage is attractive to buyers seeking to maximize the value of their equity or down payment. Owners sensitive to a buyer's needs price their businesses with this method and sell them faster.

The leveraged cash flow method is an acid test to challenge over priced business opportunities. When the price doesn't make sense, just adjust the calculation to identify a more acceptable estimate. This is an important element of an entrepreneur's negotiating skill because many businesses are overpriced. Often owners are so uncertain about how value is calculated, they establish a safeguard price that is far too high.

The LCF formula is flexible and versatile, too. It is constructed so variables are easily changed to examine different options. These may vary from market to market, business type to business type. This flexibility is needed when valuing small businesses because no two are alike.

Effective Phrase

"Show me how, by paying the asking price, the business will create enough cash flow to pay management compensation and pay off the debt."

This tough question is a direct challenge to value. Use it in preliminary investigations leading to a due diligence. It may save you a lot of time. It is particularly effective if you suspect a business is overpriced. In most cases the owner will not respond because it won't be possible – there's not enough cash flow. That's what happens when a business is overpriced. This is an opportunity. The effective phrase creates an opening to recommend an alternative price that will fulfill the intended objectives. Negotiations have begun. In certain cases, however, owners claim the needed cash flow could be available if the buyer makes the business realize its potential. Three responses to this position are available: "Would you pay this price for this business?" or, "Would you pay a price based on what exists or what might be?," or simply to say, "what you see is what you get" should be sufficient.

The Leveraged Cash Flow Method

The leveraged cash flow method of business valuation accommodates both a seller's desire for cash and a buyer's need for financing. It includes the cost of acquisition financing as a component of value. Free cash flow is used to retire debt that is routinely secured. There are two primary sources of financing. One, a bank, will offer more restrictive terms than the other, a seller. Variations in financing terms will affect the cost or amount of financing available. This in turn affects the price in such a way that one type of financing typically produces a lower value than the other. Therefore, the cash flow method of valuation is presented in two forms: one with seller financing and the other using financing from a commercial lender. Together they help build a value range based on business cash flow. Comparing values derived from the leveraged cash flow methods with the calculated capitalization and excess earnings values creates this range of values.

Seller Financing

Business owners want to sell out for the highest price, in the shortest time, for the least effort. Financing the sale to a buyer is a good way to accomplish this objective. There are other reasons owners finance businesses they sell. Financing from a bank is harder to secure; it takes longer, more disclosures are required, it's more expensive, and it drives the business value down. By comparison, seller financing is a path of less resistance and it will make the opportunity more attractive. Compared to banks, sellers also have more faith in, and a willingness to accept, tangible and intangible assets as collateral for debt. They have direct experience with the ability of these assets to produce a financial result. Seller financing provides regular monthly income, perhaps for retirement following years of building a

117

business. Also, the terms can work to the advantage of a seller. The business value might be higher. Here are factors to consider when contemplating seller financing.

Interest Rates and Terms

Interest rates for sellers who finance their property can often be the same as those charged by a local lender. This is normally acceptable to buyers unless interest rates start to rise so high that the cost of financing dramatically affects the price. Just such a situation occurred in the late 1970s and early 1980s when interest rates were as high as 20%. Business sellers took advantage of this opportunity by offering buyers a much more desirable, lower rate.

Internet Reference

http://www.federalreserve.gov

The Federal Reserve, the central bank of the United States, was founded by Congress in 1913 to provide the nation with a safer, more flexible, and more stable monetary and financial system.

Today the Federal Reserve's duties fall into four general areas: (1) conducting the nation's monetary policy; (2) supervising and regulating banking institutions and protecting the credit rights of consumers; (3) maintaining the stability of the financial system; and (4) providing certain financial services to the U.S. government, the public, financial institutions, and foreign official institutions.

Sometimes a seller will attempt to boost the sale price with substantial reductions in the interest rate charged on financing. IRS regulations set a floor on the interest rate charged in an installment sale. In these instances the IRS will treat the transaction as if a base rate of interest were charged that is greater than unstated interest collected. The effect of this treatment is a conversion of gross profit (from the sale of a business) that might have been more preferentially treated as a capital gain into ordinary income. The taxes due will be greater. These rules are complex, however, and as with all other references to Tax Code Provisions, seek advice from a qualified tax consultant.

The second financing variable to consider is the term. A general rule to help determine this variable is: "The life of the loan should be equal to or less than the service life of the asset securing the debt." Using this premise, a 10-year loan on an investment of videotapes for a video rental store might be inappropriate. Conversely, a three-year term for land with a new building is not long enough.

Businesses without real estate and including only personal property (furnishings, fixtures, equipment an inventory) are often financed for three, five or seven years. The difference is based on the business RPM, trailing and current earnings, cash flows, LTV, DCR and qualifications of the buyer.

Where real estate is used to secure the loan in addition to business personal property, the financing term is normally 15, 20 or even 30 years. Also, separate loans may be made for the real estate and one or more categories of personal property.

Like its companion variable, interest rate, the longer the term the more financing available. Yet, one would not expect a seller to be positioned holding a 30-year loan on business real estate where obsolescence can easily occur. Most common are 15-to-20-year terms or the alternative of a 30-year amortization with a 15-year due date.

Using the LCF Method

Four steps are needed to use the LCF method of valuing a business. The first is to simply retrieve free cash flow available from the ERCON performed in a due diligence. Be sure to use trailing earnings from the most current business fiscal year. If trends are strong, use a weighted value taken from two or three years past. Avoid using projected earnings since too many things can cause them to change. Also, the free cash selected will presume that an appropriate value for management compensation is considered.

In the second step, convert free cash flow into a stream of monthly payments. These will service the debt created. Divide the annual free cash flow by 12, since monthly payments are normally requested. In cases where bi-monthly, quarterly, semi-annual or annual payments are preferred, divide the free cash flow by 6, 4, 2, or 1 respectively.

Third, determine the amount of debt the free cash flow can support. (Recall the discussion of amortization as it pertains to financing.) The payment is identified in step two above. Next, the analyst will recommend a loan term, interest rate and future value at the due date of the loan (usually zero). From these four variables the loan amount is calculated. Using (or learning to use) an amortizing or financial calculator to determine loan variables is recommended.

The last step is to add equity to the loan amount – in this case a down payment that a capable buyer is willing to pay. This combination of equity and debt is business value. Here the valuation analyst's skill is crucial. (Market information is helpful.) As a rule of thumb consider the relationship of down payment to management compensation and the price paid for intangibles – goodwill. Consider the situation.

Determining Equity

It is easy to calculate debt by extrapolating free cash flow into payments on a loan using known market variables, e.g. interest rate, term, etc. Equity is determined differently.

Buyers who are buying a job tend to think of a business as a job. They favorably view business opportunities whose down payment is one to one and a half times the annual management compensation they expect to receive. This is a good benchmark for general use. In many cases business offerings request much more equity or down payment. When surveying the market for common characteristics, pay less attention to what is offered. Focus on characteristics of businesses actually sold. In any case, attractive leverage will be desirable.

Equity may vary depending on the type or capital structure of a business, as well. Small service companies with few assets and high profit margins can sell for a price equal to one year's management compensation. Very stable, asset-laden companies can command a premium, too. For them a down payment can be twice management compensation or more. In cases where business trends are unfavorable and business RPM is low, equity required to buy can be less than one year's compensation.

In determining how much equity to use, a second consideration is goodwill. Business buyers hesitate when the price for intangible assets is more than one year's management compensation. They do not like to pay too much for this type of property unless it can be demonstrated that the assets are unique and directly drive revenue. Otherwise, a benchmark to follow is that equity should not exceed the annual management compensation.

(This, too, will vary and often does when financing is shifted from the seller to a lender.)

It is possible to use business RPM (risk/price multipliers) to determine investor equity or the down payment portion of a business value. This technique will standardize the LCF method, provided market forces are well known and reasonably stable. Comparison with other investments is possible, too. The amount of equity, expressed as a percent of management compensation, might also be calculated from the following table:

CALCULATING EQUITY FROM RISK/PRICE MULTIPLES	
Business RPM	Equity
0.00 to 1.00	0% to 50%
1.01 to 2.00	51% to 75%
2.01 to 3.00	76% to 100%
3.01 to 4.00	101% to 125%
4.01 to 5.00	126% to 150%

Using the table above, if a Risk/Price Multiple is between 0 and 1.00, the equity contributed to the investment (as a down payment) will be from zero to 50% of the annual management compensation up to $15,750. In the example of BELL-Quest, Ltd., a risk/price multiple of 2.57 indicates the range of equity will be from 75% to 100% of annual management compensation – from $23,625 to $31,500. Equity may be calculated as any amount within the range.

LEVERAGED CASH FLOW METHOD[SF]
BELL-Quest, Ltd.

VARIABLES:	
Free Cash Flow	$ 19,932
RPM	2.57
Tangible Assets	$165,000
Management Compensation	$ 31,500

Step 1: Calculate Monthly Payments For Debt

Free Cash Flow	$ 19,932
(÷) Payments per period	(÷) 12
Monthly Payments	$ 1,661

Step 2: Determine Amount of Financing

Interest Rate	9.75%
Loan Term	15
Monthly Payment	$ 1,661
Balance on Due Date	0
Serviceable Debt	$156,792

Step 3: Determine Business Value

Affordable Loan Balance	$156,792
(+) Equity (Mgt. Comp. X 1.00)	$ 31,500
BUSINESS VALUE	$188,292

The RPM technique proves less helpful when market conditions are changing rapidly. Swift changes in demand for small business investments create equally swift and sometimes significant changes in business value. (Note the superscript "SF" refers to the use of seller financing. In the next chapter a similar superscript "BF" will indicate financing is secured from a bank or commercial lender.)

123

Perform a Reality Check

Once the leveraged cash flow calculation is completed, move away from the details to inspect the overall result. Does the value calculated make good sense? Four criterion may help answer this question.

✓ Realistic financing. Review basic terms of financing to ensure they are consistent with reasonable expectations of the market. Examine length of loan, interest rate and amounts of payment in relationship to free cash flow available. If inconsistent, make final adjustments and recalculate.

✓ Amount of financial leverage. The business value is the one that will attract the most investors willing to pay the price. Investors want financial leverage; opportunities that require more than 50% equity are considered less attractive.

✓ Relationship of equity to management compensation. When the down payment is greater than the annual compensation, the desirability of the investment is often reduced. As an average benchmark use a 1:1 ratio of equity to management compensation where both are equal. Higher ratios are possible with businesses that have an impressive track record of performance; those lower are not as reliable.

✓ Relationship of equity to goodwill. With the exception of proven franchises, buyers are justifiably cautious about purchasing too much goodwill. Review the amount of intangibles in the business value. When this amount exceeds the equity, a good reason should be apparent. Otherwise, the opportunity loses luster.

Feel the Power!

Many times a calculated business value can be improved with minor adjustments to variables. Here is where a conflict between the analyst's integrity and intellect occurs. A seller's desire to justify a higher price might prompt an increase in the term of financing or a reduction in the interest rate charged. The amount of financing that a fixed amount of free cash flow can support is increased to suggest the business can justify a higher price. Reducing the management compensation to increase free cash flow or raising the RPM has a similar effect. As expected, a buyer will do the opposite to reduce the investment indicated. Note the effect of the following adjustments:

Variable	Reduced	Increased
Interest Rate	Raises Value	Lowers Value
Loan Term	Lowers Value	Raises Value
Management Compensation	Raises Value	Lowers Value
Risk/Price Multiple	Lowers Value	Raises Value

For example, a seller can adjust the RPM to 4.5 very easily, since this is a subjective measure of performance. By also offering financing it is possible to lengthen the loan term to 20 years and reduce the interest rate to 9%. These adjustments produce the following results:

LEVERAGED CASH FLOW METHOD[SF] BELL-Quest, Ltd.	
VARIABLES:	
Free Cash Flow	$ 19,932
RPM	4.50
Tangible Assets	$165,000
Management Compensation	$ 31,500
Step 1: Calculate Monthly Payments For Debt	
Free Cash Flow	$ 19,932
(÷) Payments per period	(÷) 12
Monthly Payments	$ 1,661
Step 2: Determine Amount of Financing	
Interest Rate	9.00%
Loan Term	20
Monthly Payment	$ 1,661
Balance on Due Date	0
Serviceable Debt	$184,612
Step 3: Determine Business Value	
Affordable Loan Balance	$184,612
(+) Equity (Mgt. Comp. X 1.50)	$ 47,250
BUSINESS VALUE	$231,862

The adjustments to loan term and interest rate increase business value by $43,570, or 23%. In the real world of business valuation, most businesses are offered with little regard given to justification of price. On those occasions when an owner has business valuation skill, it is clearly possible to manipulate the estimate of value to suit the purpose. A reality check will help reveal the validity of adjustments made. Challenge the value.

In the higher value, terms of financing are more favorable than those previously offered. The equity appears attractive, too. At only 20% of business value, this creates financial leverage that will stimulate increased buyer interest. The amount of equity as a percent of management compensation, however, is less desirable. At 1.5 it could give buyers a reason to hesitate. Many will react by constructing their own RPM and justify a lower business value.

The biggest problem created by the adjustments lies in the relationship of price to goodwill. With tangible assets having a fair market value of $165,000, the value of goodwill is $66,150, or 2.1 times management compensation. This is very high and will be unappealing to many potential and qualified investors. Therefore, the adjusted business value, though plausible, could be counterproductive and reduce the number of interested buyers. This does not support the goal of a business owner attempting to sell.

Make adjustments to the variables to refine business value and improve its accuracy. Ensure, however, that they remain consistent with actual marketplace conditions and the expectations of the principals involved.

12

Unlocking the Vault
A Buyer With Cash is King

"CASH = CHOICE"

It is proposed that when valuing a business it is a good idea to develop a value range using the cost, market and income approaches. Combined, these are good indicators of value. When changes in financing occur, such as those illustrated in the latter part of the previous chapter, business values often change.

While most businesses that actually sell often involve some amount of seller financing, many do not. The alternative? Pay cash or seek financing elsewhere. As long as entrepreneurs believe in the benefits of financial leverage, commercial lending institutions will remain a viable option.

Internet Reference

www.sba.gov
The U.S. Small Business Administration provides financial, technical and management assistance to help Americans start, run, and grow their businesses. The SBA is the nation's largest single financial backer of small businesses.

http://sbs.dnb.com
Dun & Bradstreet Small Business Solutions web site provides business owners with a suite of online tools to make better credit decision.

The U.S. Small Business Administration (SBA) is a branch of government established to assist entrepreneurs in most aspects of business start-up, expansion or acquisition. Small business valuation emphasizes financing. Providing services to meet this need is at the core of the SBA's mission. Its activities are varied, however, and support entrepreneurs in other ways as well (e.g., through the Service Corps of Retired Executives – or SCORE – which includes more than 12,400 counselors in 389 chapters nationwide).

Business loans typically involve greater risk than real estate loans. This is because financial benefits and value are a derivative of tangible and intangible assets. Both can evaporate quickly, diminishing their desirability when used as collateral to secure a loan. To encourage lenders to accept the greater risk of financing small businesses, the U.S. Small Business Administration (SBA) offers, under certain conditions, guarantees of payment to lenders making small business loans. Because these programs reduce risk to both the borrower and lender, they increase the desirability of small business loans. When sellers want cash for a business and buyers want to preserve financial leverage, commercial lenders get involved and, when they do, so does the SBA.

SBA 7(a) Loan Guarantee Program

Under the SBA 7(a) loan program the SBA guarantees up to $1 million of financing. Small loans carry a maximum guarantee of 85 percent. Loans are considered small if the gross amount is $150,000 or less. For loans greater than $150,000, the maximum guaranty is 75 percent.

Eligibility

The vast majority of businesses are eligible for financial assistance from the SBA. Applicant businesses must be operated for profit; be engaged in, or propose to do business in, the United States or its possessions; have reasonable owner equity to invest; and use alternative financial resources first, including personal assets. It should be noted that some businesses are ineligible for financial assistance.

Size of Businesses Eligible

The Small Business Act defines an eligible small business as one that is independently owned and operated and not dominant in its field of operation. The Act also states that in determining what is a small business, the definition shall vary from industry to industry to adequately reflect industry differences. The SBA has therefore developed size standards that define the maximum size of an eligible small business.

As the following general description of SBA's size standards demonstrates, most businesses are considered small. These represent general definitions, however, that in some cases are further defined by a specific Standard Industrial Classification (SIC) code.

Retail and Service	$3.5 to $13.5 Million
Construction	$7.0 to $17.0 Million
Agriculture	$0.5 to $3.5 Million
Wholesale	No more than 100 employees
Manufacturing	500 to 1,500 employees

131

If a potential borrower is close to these standards, size eligibility should be discussed with the local SBA office. Also note that the standards for a particular business may change from time to time and some exceptions do apply.

Use of Proceeds

In general, SBA 7(a) Loans may be made for a variety of reasons. These include the purchase of real estate to house the business operations; construction, renovation or leasehold improvements; acquisition of furniture, fixtures, machinery and equipment; purchase of inventory; and working capital. They may not be used to finance floor plan needs, to purchase real estate held for investment, to pay delinquent or withholding taxes, or to pay existing debt unless it can be shown that the refinancing will benefit the small business and that the need to refinance is not indicative of imprudent management. Certain other special considerations apply to the types of businesses and applicants eligible for SBA loan programs.

Subject to certain conditions, SBA 7(a) Loans for a Change of Business Ownership are possible, provided the business benefits from the change. In most cases, this benefit should be seen in promoting the sound development of the business or, perhaps, in preserving its existence.

SBA Loan Maturities

SBA loan programs are generally intended to encourage longer term small business financing, but actual loan maturities are based on the ability to repay, the purpose of the loan proceeds, and the useful life of the assets financed. Maximum loan maturities have been established: 25 years for real estate and equipment and, generally, seven years for working capital.

Loans for working capital purposes will not exceed seven years, except when a longer maturity (up to 10 years) may be needed to ensure repayment. The maximum maturity of loans used to finance fixed assets other than real estate will be limited to the economic life of those assets – but in no instance exceed 25 years. The 25-year maximum will generally apply to the acquisition of land and buildings or the refinancing of debt incurred in their acquisition. Where business premises are to be constructed or significantly renovated, the 25-year maximum would be in addition to the time needed to complete construction. (Significant renovation means construction of at least one-third of the current value of the property.)

Interest Rates

Interest rates are negotiated between the borrower and the lender but are subject to SBA maximums, which are pegged to the Prime Rate.

Interest rates may be fixed or variable. Fixed rate loans of $50,000 or more must not exceed Prime Plus 2.25 percent if the maturity is less than seven years, and Prime Plus 2.75 percent if the maturity is or more.

For loans between $25,000 and $50,000, maximum rates must not exceed Prime Plus 3.25 percent if the maturity is less than seven years, and Prime Plus 3.75 percent if the maturity is seven years or more.

For loans of $25,000 or less, the maximum interest rate must not exceed Prime Plus 4.25 percent if the maturity is less than seven years, and Prime Plus 4.75 percent, if the maturity is seven years or more.

Variable loans may be pegged to either the lowest prime rate or the SBA optional peg rate. The optional peg rate is a weighted average of the rates the federal government pays for loans with maturities similar to the average SBA loan. It is calculated quarterly and published in the "Federal Register." The lender and the borrower negotiate the amount of the spread, which will be added to the base rate. An adjustment period is selected which will identify the frequency at which the note rate will change. It must be no more often than monthly and must be consistent.

Fees on SBA Loans

To offset the cost of the SBA's loan programs to the taxpayer, the Agency charges lenders a guarantee and a servicing fee for each loan approved. These fees can be passed on to the borrower once the lender has paid them. The amount of the fees is determined by the amount of the loan guaranty.

Effective December 22, 2000, when the loan amount is $150,000 or less, the guaranty fee will be 2 percent of the guaranteed portion. Lenders are permitted to retain 25 percent of this fee (50 basis points). This is only applicable to loans of $150,000 or less. For loans more than $150,000 up to and including $700,000, a 3 percent guaranty fee will be charged. For loans greater than $700,000, a 3.5 percent guaranty fee will be charged.

In addition, all loans will be subject to a 50 basis point (0.5%) annualized servicing fee, which is applied to the outstanding balance of SBA's guaranteed portion of the loan.

Processing fees, origination fees, application fees, points, brokerage fees, bonus points, and other fees that could be charged to an SBA loan applicant are prohibited.

Prepayment

Effective for all loans where applications were received by the lender on or after December 22, 2000, a new prepayment charge paid by the borrower to the SBA ("subsidy recoupment fee") has been added for those loans that meet the following criteria:

✓ have a maturity of 15 years or more where the borrower is prepaying voluntarily;

✓ the prepayment amount exceeds 25 percent of the outstanding balance of the loan; AND

✓ the prepayment is made within the first 3 years after the date of the first disbursement of the loan proceeds.

The prepayment fee calculation is as follows:

✓ during the first year after disbursement, 5 percent of the amount of the prepayment;

✓ during the second year after the disbursement, 3 percent of the amount of the prepayment; or

✓ during the third year after disbursement, 1 percent of the amount of prepayment.

Certified/Preferred SBA Lenders

Banks make small business loans and the SBA guarantees them. The most active and expert participating lenders qualify for SBA's streamlined lending programs. Under these programs, lenders are delegated partial or full authority to approve loans, which results in faster service from the SBA. This can be a crucial factor when a quick turnaround time is needed to satisfy an aggressive acquisition timetable.

Certified lenders are those who have been heavily involved in regular SBA loan-guaranty processing and have met certain other criteria. They receive a partial delegation of authority and are given a three-day turnaround time by the SBA on their applications. Certified lenders account for nearly a third of all SBA loan guaranties.

Preferred lenders are chosen from SBA's best lenders and enjoy full delegation of lending authority in exchange for a lower rate of guaranty. This lending authority must be renewed at least every two years, and the SBA examines the lender's portfolio periodically. Preferred loans account for more than 10 percent of SBA loans.

SBA LowDoc Loan Program

These loans are available to borrowers of $150,000 or less. The LowDoc features a revised one-page application form that is the same for all LowDoc loans regardless of dollar amount, reducing the burden of paperwork for borrower and lender. If approved, the SBA will guarantee a maximum of 85 percent of the loan and provide a 36-hour turnaround time to the lender. Eligible businesses must have fewer than 100 employees; average annual sales in the preceding three years must not exceed $5 million for the business, including affiliates; the business and its owners must have good credit; and the business owners must be of good character.

SBAExpress

This program encourages lenders to make small loans to small businesses. Participating lenders use their documentation and procedures to approve, service and liquidate loans of up to $150,000. In return, the SBA provides a rapid response – within 36 hours of receiving the completed application - and up to 50% guaranty on the loan. SBAExpress lenders can also offer revolving lines of credit to borrowers with this program.

Prequalification Pilot Loan Program

This program uses intermediaries to assist prospective borrowers in developing viable loan application packages and securing loans.

Once the loan package is assembled, it is submitted to the SBA for expedited consideration; a decision usually is made within three days. If the application is approved, the SBA issues a letter of prequalification stating the SBA's intent to guarantee the loan. The maximum amount for loans under the program is $250,000; the SBA will guarantee up to 85 percent for loans up to and including $150,000, and 75 percent for loans over $150,000. The intermediary (usually a Small Business Development Center) then helps the borrower locate a lender offering the most competitive rates.

Small Business Development Centers serving as intermediaries do not charge a fee for loan packaging. For-profit organizations will charge a fee.

Bank versus Seller Financing

A key difference exists between bank versus seller financing when using the leveraged cash flow method of business valuation. With the latter, the amount of financing is determined from loan terms and the amount of debt the business can afford. Typically 100% of free cash flow is committed to retire debt. Sellers are not so concerned about the relationship between debt and the market value of tangible assets serving as collateral.

Bank guidelines are more costly and challenging. These establish the upper limit of credit available to a small business borrower without regard to free cash flow. Debt is determined using loan-to-value and debt-coverage ratios, explained earlier in this text. When combined with other factors such as interest rate and terms on financing available, a bank lends less than a seller. In some cases, the amount of free cash flow committed to service debt is also less. When this happens, the difference between free cash flow and annual debt service (ADS) on a bank loan may be diverted to pay off a smaller second mortgage to a seller. (Bankers often view the existence of such as a vote of confidence in the buyer from the seller; it can be an important incentive to lenders whose loan approval is wavering.)

To illustrate the immediate impact of bank lending guidelines on available financing, consider the following example.

Loan-to-Value Ratio:	80% for all assets with an SBA Guaranty
Debt-Coverage Ratio:	1.2
Assets Market Value:	$165,000
Free Cash Flow:	$19,932

With this information a maximum loan available can be determined. To do so, multiply the assets market value by the loan-to-value ratio.

$165,000 x 80% = $132,000 (maximum loan available)

Next, convert free cash flow into annual debt service when discounted by the bank's debt-coverage ratio. This is done as follows:

$19,932 ÷ 1.2 = $16,610 (annual debt service)

Divide the annual debt service figure by 12 to determine the monthly debt service. Apply the monthly payment calculated ($1,384.17) to the terms negotiated in order to calculate the loan amount affordable. Assume the interest rate is 9.75% and the loan term is 15 years. Here are the variables used with an amortizing calculator to determine the loan amount.

Payment	$ 1,384.17
Interest Rate	9.75%
Term	15
Future Value	0
Loan Amount	$130,660

Since the bank has set a debt ceiling of $132,000, the loan amount ($130,660) is affordable and should be acceptable. Notice, however, additional free cash flow still exists – the difference between business free cash flow and annual debt service on bank financing. In some cases, sellers refuse to accept any financing. When this occurs, many often treat the excess free cash flow as added compensation to the buyer. A like amount is added to equity requirements. More frequently, however, the excess free cash flow can pay the costs of a junior lien to a seller in those cases where the bank does not object. The amount of excess free cash flow is calculated as:

$19,932 - $16,610 = $3,322 (excess free cash flow)

Junior liens from sellers typically cost more. The interest is higher and terms are shorter than senior liens by comparison. Assume the following conditions of a junior lien.

Payment	$ 276.83
Interest Rate	10.00%
Term	7
Future Value	0
Loan Amount	$16,675

Complete the financing option of leveraged cash flow valuation with bank financing by combining both loans with a down payment. Use the same business RPM indicating a 1:1 ratio of equity to management compensation.

$130,660 (senior lien)
+ $16,675 (junior lien)
+ $31,500 (equity)
―――――――――――
= $178,835 (value)

The comparison to seller financing reveals the impact of a bank loan. Value is reduced by about five percent.

LCF/Seller Financing	$188,292
LCF/Bank Financing	<$178,835>
Difference	$ 9,457

The completed leveraged cash flow method using a bank-financing option follows.

LEVERAGED CASH FLOW^{BF}
BELL-QUEST, LTD.

Variables

Free Cash Flow	$19,932
Management Compensation	31,500
Tangible Assets	165,000
RPM	2.57
DCR	1.2
LTV	80%

Step 1: Calculate Monthly Payments for Debt

Business Free Cash Flow	$ 19,932
(÷) Payments per period	12
Monthly Payments	$,1661

Step 2: Determine Amount of Financing

	1st Mortgage	2nd Mortgage
Interest Rate	9.75%	10.00%
Loan Term	15	7
Monthly Payment	$ 1,384.17	$ 276.83
Balance on Due Date	0	0
Serviceable Debt	$ 130,660	$16,675

STEP 3: Determine Business Value

Total Financing Affordable	$147,335.00
(+)Equity (Mgt. Comp. * 1.00)	$ 31,500.00
BUSINESS VALUE	$178,835.00

13

Investors Raise A Challenge to Buy Low

"When negotiating, the best logic usually wins."

Situation Analysis

Limited knowledge of business value is a hindrance to negotiations. Sellers discourage buyers when they over price their businesses. Buyers offend sellers when they offer half what the business is worth. Either strategy may prevail – and often does - because both are uncertain about the actual business value. Neither is acting logically nor could mount a capable defense of their position. No real progress comes from either approach.

Using business valuation skill is a logical approach that can be used to justify an offer. This can be a terrific advantage for investors who want to buy low without creating a feud.

You Make Your Money When You Buy

Entrepreneurs make money when they buy, *and* when they sell. Buying low has many advantages. It is possible to sell out quickly and recoup most or all of the original investment. The difference between acquisition cost and actual value is an immediate profit. It isn't necessary to spend years building added business value to create added wealth. Some people pay so much that the business they buy cannot be sold to recover their investment for years, if ever. It takes patience, AND the ability to recognize a good value or create one with counter proposals. Every business has its price.

Effective Phrase

"I'll make an offer but I always pay less than market value."

This is an effective way to open negotiations with sellers. It reduces their expectations so they are not surprised or alienated. It suggests that, in the past, other sellers have sold below market value to this buyer who has obviously performed. Plus, it gives sellers a measure of control. They can choose to proceed and hear the offer or not. It is also a test of the sellers' confidence in their business value. Most, out of sheer curiosity, will always want to know what you have in mind. The door is open.

Business valuation skill empowers buyers, sellers and the acquisition process. Core issues are confronted head-on. When both parties understand how business value is calculated, it is easier to close the gap between buyer and seller positions, yet the high-spirited competition and negotiations can remain lively and fair. The final outcome is a win-win transaction.

The often-quoted statistic that four out of five business start-ups fail means an equal number of owners fail, too. Their errors begin before a business is acquired. By addressing certain essentials, however, the potential for success improves.

✓ Understand non-negotiables.

✓ Know what a target property is worth.

✓ Communicate value to encourage acceptance.

Non-Negotiables

Buyer know thyself. It is unwise to have unrealistic expectations. Moreover, recognizing critical factors of success helps prevent trouble before it begins. Observing non-negotiables is one way this is accomplished. Non-negotiables are things the entrepreneur cannot do without. To do so makes failure a near certainty. Following are non-negotiables for every buyer's list.

Don't pay too much. Entrepreneurs who start, buy or exchange into a business make this their mantra for life. It is never knowingly violated. When it is, the path to poor results is already underfoot. After learning effective valuation techniques, how could this occur? Adrenaline is powerful. When a live business candidate emerges, the rush of excitement is persuasive enough to overpower reason. It's easy for the heart to overrule the head. Business valuation techniques help restore a healthy balance and prevent mistakes.

Remember the Objective

Many entrepreneurs forget to consider an important issue when acquiring a business: Business owners do well and do best when doing what they like most. They have to, because entrepreneurs must be willing to work 16 hours a day for themselves instead of eight hours for someone else. It's not worth the effort, however, if there's no profit in the mix. Buying low ensures this mix is available.

Financial autonomy is the goal. Business is the impetus of the American system of free enterprise. Business ownership is the mechanism entrepreneurs choose to accomplish their goals. Performance leads to profit. Profit leads to choice. Choices lead to freedom. In this quest, business valuation skills offer a useful tool.

Plan to Shop

There are many businesses available for purchase. Some are good opportunities – others are among the four out of five heading for failure. There must be a compelling reason to acquire a business whose trend of trailing revenue and earnings is declining. Instead, find the business that is thriving, surviving or can be reenergized by identifying and scaling a growth wall in the path of progress. Financial autonomy has a better chance of occurring when a business shows a favorable track record.

Good business opportunities are often overpriced. Sifting through all the opportunities, both good and bad, to find the best value is the goal. But this can be time-consuming, and entrepreneurs are pressed for time. So, the objective of smart buyers is to know what information to ask for, and to ask for it early. The key ingredients of the due diligence provide clues to accomplishing this.

First Impressions

Buyers cannot construct an offer involving a commitment of financial resources without knowing what benefits and income go with the property. That is like buying a property "sight unseen," and it's unwise. Buyers should not be expected to make offers based on innuendo, business potential and the romance of ownership. They are well advised and rewarded when their focus remains fixed on the economic rewards available.

Conversely, sellers can't be expected to open the books to every buyer expressing a casual interest. Serious intent should be demonstrated. Otherwise requests for financial disclosures are met with resistance, and rightly so - buyers could be competitors in disguise, attempting to pick the seller's pockets for competitive intelligence. Requests for an executed non-disclosure agreement may be premature, however. The trick is to find out if both buyer and seller are in the same ballpark.

Consider the power of first impressions. With people they can be revealing and accurate. In fact, everything afterward is an attempt to confirm what is already intuitively known. Business opportunities are similar. It isn't necessary to perform a due diligence to develop a quick opinion of business value. Using basic variables and three valuation strategies help form a reasonably accurate first impression.

Key Information

Most sellers know how to run their business. Don't assume they know how to determine what it's worth or how to sell it. This is a buyer's advantage IF the buyer takes the initiative. To do this requires the buyer to take control of the acquisition process and lead the way to the closing table. Simple questions can be very effective tools.

Challenge the Price

Always counter offer an asking price. Always. This is a seller's opening gambit, and never to be accepted without a challenge. Occasionally a business is available but no price is stated. This is typically the result of a seller who: 1) doesn't know the value of the property, 2) hopes to find a buyer who doesn't know the value of the property either, 3) has a high standard of confidentiality or 4) is skilled enough in valuation and negotiating techniques to know better. The clue to determining the skill of the seller can be revealed with the question, "How was the business value

147

determined?" The answer received will reveal the seller's skill and negotiating capability. If it is consistent with any of the first three cases just mentioned, it is difficult to proceed very far. Financial disclosures will be equally limited. Don't invest too much time. If it appears the seller fits the fourth category, deliver a non-disclosure agreement – this could be a good business, so look closely.

Challenge the Terms

"Are you willing to finance any portion of the asking price?" This is an excellent question to test the sellers' confidence in their business. It also helps buyers get a fix on factors motivating a seller to sell. Generally speaking, the word "terms" means financing and its conditions. For reasons described earlier, financing provided by a seller is more attractive to most buyers. Where seller financing is not available, the buyer needs a good knowledge of loan criteria from potential commercial lenders. Investment leverage in business acquisitions can improve the financial return. It will be important to consider the cost to service debt from business cash flow. This is something else a buyer needs to know early.

Challenge the Assets

"What do I get for my money?" is a simple question that challenges sellers and tests their confidence in business value. Typically, responses describe the various assets included in the business and their market value. Goodwill, if it exists, is difficult for sellers to include. This approach allows a buyer to add asset values and see if their collective total matches the business price. In this process any price paid for goodwill is revealed. The subtle challenge to a price continues setting the stage to buy low.

The question about assets has another benefit. Buyers need to know the type and amount of collateral available to secure financing from a bank. It puts a seller on the defensive by challenging the asking price of property being sold.

Challenge the Revenue, EBIT and Cash Flow

A request for details like revenue, EBIT and cash flow threatens a seller more than broad-based inquiries. Knowing business revenue, however, is about as broad as it can get and shouldn't create unfavorable exposure. More importantly, getting revenue opens the door to inquire about trailing revenue that reveals business trends, which is important to the valuation process.

EBIT (earnings before interest and taxes) is a little more difficult to secure. Remember, sellers maximize expenses to minimize taxable earnings. Recognize also that sellers understand this because they are doing it. The problem is they may not be able to articulate it confidently, or precisely, to buyers. So ask, "I realize there is a difference between net profit and cash flow. Can you tell me what the business earnings are before interest and taxes?" This question signals a seller that you understand what he does but can't come right out and say it. Everybody knows that in business it's not what the business earns that counts – it's what ownership gets to keep. That information is more private.

The question just asked has a second benefit. It sets the stage to develop an "estimate" of business cash flow. It is easy to follow up with a request for additional limited information. "Was there a depreciation expense, a salary for your management effort, too?," is a great follow-up. Creating added interest advances the inquiry. Every seller wants to create more interest. Recall the shortcut offered earlier in this book that described how entrepreneurs quickly size up a business. Add a request for monthly cash expenses and, if received, estimate the business's cash flow.

Challenge the Management Compensation

Most buyers know how much income from employment they need to support their lifestyle. It is always helpful to know what existing ownership believes management compensation should be. This is not a threatening request. Compare answers to the employment income tables in the U.S. Department of Labor Website. They can confirm estimates made and provide the basis to challenge them.

Challenge the Price with Capitalization

Buyers who accept a business asking price let sellers to do their thinking for them. This is a lazy, dangerous approach and very easy to avoid with the right skill. It pays to be a skeptic. Buyers demonstrate a healthy sense of skepticism by challenging representations made, such as the asking price. This is the easiest and most obvious way to negotiate a lower sales price. The reason more buyers don't take this approach is because they are unable to use valuation techniques to justify a different position – they have nothing on which to base an argument. For this reason, business valuation becomes a powerful tool.

The simplest way to challenge an asking price is by subjecting it to a capitalization method of determining business value. Assume the following from the example of BELL-Quest, Ltd., used in previous chapters:

✓ Asking price: $300,000

✓ Terms: 25% equity with seller financing for 15 years at 10% ($2,417.86 monthly)

✓ Market value of tangible assets: $165,000

✓ Revenue: $608,951

✓ Net Profit: $21,920

150

✓ Cash Flow: $51,442

✓ Management compensation: $31,500

✓ Business Capitalization Rate: 11.5%

Begin the price challenge by using variables provided by the seller - price and cash flow – to figure the rate of return. Free cash flow is $19,932 (cash flow of $51,432 minus $31,500 management compensation). The equation to determine the rate of return (Free cash flow divided by the asking price) becomes:

$$\underline{\$19,932} \qquad = .0664 \text{ or } 6.64\% \text{ rate of return}$$

At the asking price of $300,000 the rate of return to an investor is 6.64%. This is less than the expected capitalization rate of 11.5%. At the asking price, the business does not offer a competitive rate of return. This is not good news to a seller.

**"If you back a seller into a corner,
be prepared to show them
a trap door to the treasure chamber."**

Now, calculate the amount of income that should be available from an investment of $300,000 producing the expected rate of return. Substitute an 11.5% capitalization rate and recalculate:

.115 (11.5%) X $300,000   = $34,500 (free cash flow)

151

To produce the desired capitalization rate the income (free cash flow) should be $34,500. The actual amount is $19,932 or 42% less, based on market indicators of performance. This is another indication the business is overpriced.

Finally, calculate the adjusted current business value by using current free cash flow and the expected capitalization rate:

$$\frac{\$19,932}{.115 \ (11.5\%)} = \$173,322 \text{ (adjusted sales value)}$$

Based on these criteria, a buyer can determine <u>the business is overpriced by roughly $125,000.</u>

Effective Phrase

"Would you be willing to pay that for this business?"

The analysis and question is fast, easy and revealing. Wide discrepancies in asking price and value are commonplace. With this information the buyer now can terminate the inquiry or, if the only apparent problem with the business is the price, attempt to negotiate it lower. In either case time and money can be saved.

Another productive approach is to ask the seller to explain how the price of $300,000 was constructed, or request additional information to shed new light on the issue. This yields valuable information. In the absence of meaningful evidence or willingness to listen to reason, don't waste too much time. Move on.

Challenge the Price with Excess Earnings

A second way to challenge the asking price is by applying the excess earnings method to confirm a business asking price. A business RPM (risk/price multiple) is needed. This is difficult to do without the benefit of a due diligence. Circumvent the process (early in the inquiry) by interviewing the seller. Explain how an RPM is created and ask the seller to assign a simple value of zero-to-five to each basic category used to build an RPM. These can be challenged later if a due diligence indicates a need for adjustments.

If a seller is unwilling to provide this assistance, the buyer can make a general estimate of the values leading to an RPM. Bear in mind, however, this means a seller is showing an unwillingness to even talk about the business they want to sell. Their motivation may not be very high.

Begin with variables that are known or can be calculated from what is given. Free cash flow is $19,932 and market value of tangible assets is $165,000. First calculate the value of excess earnings using the asking price and value of tangible assets included in the business offering:

$300,000 - $165,000   = $135,000 (excess earnings)

The asking price thus includes $135,000 for excess earnings or goodwill. Next calculate the RPM needed to support this investment. Recall, excess earnings are the same as free cash flow. Working backwards to calculate a business RPM is easily accomplished.

$$\frac{\$\,135{,}000}{\$\,19{,}932} = 6.77 \text{ (risk/price multiple)}$$

A 6.77 business RPM is off the scale that measures small business performance. It could only occur in a very hot seller's market or when a business has almost no margin for error or risk. The exceptions are very fast-growing companies in a hot industry that offer lots of synergy in a consolidation acquisition. Few businesses - if any - are so devoid of investment uncertainty. At this point the buyer can ask the seller, "How is $135,000 for goodwill justified?" Based on the response received terminate the analysis or, as before, indicate the need for evidence to support use of such a high business RPM.

Challenge the Price with Leveraged Cash Flow

Leveraged cash flow is the acid test of business value. Other measures of value are good, but this challenge measures the investor's ability to afford the price. It is very telling. To complete this challenge one must know the cash flow and cost of debt service, which as offered, is $2,417.86 per month or $29,014 per year. Calculate management compensation:

$51,432 - $29,014   = $22,418
(cash flow for management compensation)

Perform a sanity check. Financial leverage is good, since the seller offers the business for 25% down ($75,000). Management compensation is deficient to expectations by

$9,082, or 29%. This is a problem because it may not enable buyers to support a reasonable lifestyle. That would disqualify the business as an investment candidate. The relationship of equity ($75,000) to management compensation ($22,418), 3.3 to 1, is also out of balance when compared to small business benchmarks. Finally, the goodwill at $135,000 is 1.8 times equity and 6 times management compensation. This business price is too high for expectations. Ask the seller, "Would you run this business for the compensation available while paying $135,000 for goodwill?"

Reversing roles is the easiest way to convey the desirability of the seller's asking price. It helps make sellers more flexible. If it appears the seller is willing to listen to alternatives, illustrate a price that makes sense. If the seller remains inflexible, walk away. *And never, ever bluff.* Too much is at stake to play games. Say what you mean and mean what you say.

To calculate the best price using the leveraged cash flow approach, return to the previous equation and subtract management compensation from cash flow. The remainder is free cash flow that can be used to service debt. This substitution of management compensation for debt service ensures that the buyers' personal service income needs can be met. Next, divide free cash flow by the number of payments made per year (12) on financing. This is the monthly payment available to service debt. Then recalculate the present value of the debt using the monthly payment. This reveals the amount of financing the business can afford to pay. Finally, in the absence of a business RPM to calculate a down payment, use a common benchmark to determine this amount – one year's management compensation.

Notice the use of a 10% interest rate on financing (as proposed) instead of a lower 9.75% market rate. This appears to be a compromise to the seller, but it actually advances the buyer's cause by reducing the amount of financing and, therefore, the price.

LEVERAGED CASH FLOW CHALLENGE BELL-QUEST, LTD.	
Step 1	
Cash Flow	$ 51,432
Management Compensation	< 31,500.00>
Step 2	
Free Cash Flow	19,932
(÷) Payments per year	12
Periodic Payments Available	1,661
Step 3	
Term:	15 years
Rate:	10.00%
Payment:	$ 1,661.79
Future Value	0
Loan Amount	$ 154,568.41
Step 4	
Loan Amount	$ 154,568.41
Equity	$ 31,500.00
Business Value	$ 186,068.41

Notice the value indicated is $2,223.59 less than the value calculated earlier ($188,292) using the LCF method. The variance is created by a slightly higher interest rate on financing. A formidable challenge can be presented to ownership's offering price of $300,000.

The Right Price

The shrewdest investors follow the simplest approach. They identify the price at which the business value meets their expectations. They communicate their position clearly and firmly. Then they stick to their value and negotiate – giving away things that don't really matter. In each case the result is the same. Profit is earned the day ownership is transferred.

Entrepreneurs following these strategies know they do not need to buy every business to be successful. Be patient. Wait for a good opportunity. It is only important to invest in good values. A business purchased for the right price can produce enough profit to compensate entrepreneurs for months or a year's worth of earnings. It is worth waiting for. A bad deal can be equally costly and is worse than no deal at all.

14

Sellers Rise To A Challenge And Gain Control

"Never let anyone put you on defense."

Control of the acquisition process is all-important. Buyers attempt to wrest it away from sellers with challenging questions they think sellers are unprepared to answer. They will put a seller on the defensive. If possible uncertainty grows. The seller becomes more malleable – willing to adjust their price. This is costly. Advance planning and preparing good answers is the best way to take control of negotiations.

To avoid selling too low, successful sellers and brokers prepare to deal with the expected and unexpected aspects of selling a business. It can be a complex process but achieves good results.

Begin by preparing answers to questions a well-informed buyer may ask. Many were presented in the previous chapter. Here are effective counter phrases to use while putting in motion the all-important strategy of taking the lead. Remember, no single question will make the sale. Work instead to improve the percentages – the chance – that a sale will occur. Here are ten common questions buyers ask and effective phrases that counter them.

Request #1 - "I'll make an offer but I always pay less than market value." The best response is "That's fine, and I'm free to accept or decline." This approach is a signal the seller is open to everything but not weak to accept anything. Keep in mind, to a buyer, less than market value could be ten percent less. That might be a good opportunity. Find out what the buyer has in mind before turning them away by showing a lack of confidence.

Request #2 - Respond to the question, "Are you willing to finance any portion of the asking price?" with, "It's possible with a good offer from a qualified buyer." This tells buyers they will be expected to make disclosures, too. A credit report and financial statement are the most common. If these are not acceptable, and buyers know it, they fade quickly.

If financing is not a possibility the better response is "We had not planned to offer any financing. Local banks are available to provide that." This doesn't exclude financing as a possibility. It diverts the buyer inquiry to an alternative source. Exercise caution when suggesting other sources of financing. If you elect to provide any contacts, suggest several without making a recommendation.

Request #3 - "Give me nickels and dimes." This is a metaphor to illustrate the way some buyers won't relent in their requests for small concessions. This can start in the first meeting. Sellers who respond by agreeing to "this then that" place themselves at risk. Individually these items may have little value. Collectively, and when combined with a low offer, they can add up to a princely sum. Buyers will take the position that the seller also has "already agreed to" the concessions, to make things more difficult.

Respond to requests for numerous small concessions, "We are happy to discuss that in negotiations." This indicates a willingness to discuss the proposition but requires that the buyer show more cards - go farther into the process - to get an answer. In other words, "get serious or get lost." The more they investigate the more they will sell themselves - get emotionally involved with the business. Asking for little concessions will be harder, especially if the price is well justified.

Request #4 - "What do I get for my money" should prompt the immediate response, "Income, assets and a marketing opportunity – what any good business offers." Only a continued investigation to develop information describing each – a due diligence - will provide the answer. This is a process any seller can control to gain a negotiating advantage. Release information judiciously.

Request #5 - "Can you tell me what the business earns before interest and taxes?" is a question to describe business earning power – a key issue. Answer with revenue, net profit and EBIT. Emphasize favorable business trends if they exist. Don't rely too much on describing potential unless tangible evidence to support increases in performance already exists. This is a good occasion to counter with questions about the buyer's capability – "How much of an investment do you have available to use?" is an excellent follow-up response.

Request #6 - "How did you arrive at the asking price?" Challenges to price are all avoided when the business value is realistic. The best response will indicate value is a function of estimates using a market, cost and income approach. Do not, however, share these estimates with a buyer at this stage. The ability to do their own "homework" is an indication of their capability. Lead the way. Then, make the business available by soliciting offers. This gives buyers a sense of freedom to set their own price but challenges them to stay honest.

Request #7 - "Can I look at your books." This is a common request buyers make to ensure they are not wasting their time. It's reasonable but usually premature. Respond with, "I'm happy to offer them as a condition of an acceptable offer. Until then, know they will verify my comments." This keeps discussions moving forward and engenders confidence while bypassing the issue until a full review of the books is warranted. This also is a good occasion to mention that, in exchange for a look at the books, buyers will need to provide a signed Non-Disclosure Agreement and, perhaps, their financial statement. It keeps them honest.

Request#8 - "Will you discount for cash or take less?" Many buyers use this as way to test a seller's confidence in the business value and set the stage for a low offer. For example, a buyer might establish that the price will be less because they plan to offer cash. Then when the offer is tendered it includes seller financing, but at the cash price. A good way to handle this is by saying, "I'm happy to react to anything you care to propose in writing." This avoids suggesting a lower offer is acceptable and forces buyers to perform if they want more information.

Request #9 - "How much are you skimming?" There's only one answer, "None." Skimming is illegal. Any answer damages the credibility needed to create confidence a buyer must have to buy the business.

Request #10 - "Why are you selling?" This is a good question all buyers should ask. Unprepared sellers can offer an answer that may reveal serious weaknesses and place them at a negotiating disadvantage. That's what the buyer wants. There are many correct answers but one of the best is, "To cash in my equity and reinvest elsewhere." This is a strong answer that fits many situations and suggests the seller is not in a distressed situation.

Selling high also involves other preparations that can favorably affect negotiations. Here are several areas to address.

Conduct a Due Diligence

Sellers can control the negotiation process by controlling the information. One way is to anticipate a buyer's reaction to the business by performing a due diligence prior to a sale. Material in this book is intended to help readers do this themselves. There are three objectives to consider.

First, identify the business strengths and weaknesses. This helps guide the effort to reinforce problem areas. It also points out benefits sellers sometimes do not see, which can be emphasized in a sales marketing plan.

Second, performing a due diligence improves objectivity and expectations. This will be especially true if the opinions of others are solicited confidentially. A list of consultants whose input may be valuable includes professionals already serving the business (i.e., accountant, lawyer, insurance agent, and banker). They do not always need to know the purpose of the due diligence. It can be positioned as an annual review. Their unbiased remarks help sellers see their business for what it really is.

Third, the due diligence will include developing of a business RPM. This can be used to calculate value with the excess earnings and leveraged cash flow methods of business valuation. That is a key benefit. Additionally, an RPM constructed under these low stress conditions is likely to be better considered, objective and accurate. That is an important resource when a buyer challenges it with one of his or her own.

These preparations are part of an overall strategy that does not give a buyer a reason to say "no." When the time comes, this advance preparation will help a seller stay focused on running the business while negotiating its sale. Maintaining a calm, confident and organized state of mind at that time is sure to be perceived as strength.

Price

Price is on thing over which sellers have total control. The extra effort to prepare a business for sale pays big dividends in a price that can be substantiated and received. It takes time to do this job right, but the work is small compared to the years of work it takes to build the business. That is all of little value without a final effort to maximize the wealth created. Preparation is the key. This aspect for the seller's consideration is most important and, fortunately, the one over which sellers have the most control.

When developing a business price in anticipation of a sale, several things are up for discussion. The objective is to weigh the following elements carefully and create an attractive offering.

A Seller's Biggest Mistake

Don't overprice the property. History indicates that uncertainty about business value often drives up asking prices. This is a reaction to the fear of selling for too little. Leaving "room to negotiate" is not an unreasonable tactic until the room becomes the size of a gymnasium. This strategy then creates more damage than it was designed to avoid. An unrealistic price cannot stand up against the sound logic of a well-informed buyer with penetrating questions.

Overpricing a property discourages buyers from pursuing an inquiry beyond the initial phase. Lots of good inquiries lead to attractive selling options. With fewer buyers in tow, options are limited. The inclination is to take "whatever is available" and an unreasonably strong position quickly softens. The consequence is sellers are easily placed on the defensive, and the outcome can be a sale of the business below market.

Best Time to Sell

The bulk of this book is designed to build valuation skill. The question of "how much" is easily answered, but "when to sell" is another question of some importance. It has an easy answer too. The best time to sell a business is just before its value reaches a peak. Knowing your marketplace and your business provides clues to when the peak will arrive. Unfortunately, this also is when most sellers refuse to let go. By this act they could be letting go of a capital gain from a sale whose economic value could be greater than another two or three years of business income taxed at ordinary income rates.

Prior to a business peak, all systems are go. Trends are positive, as trailing revenue and earnings are steadily increasing. The business enjoys a high profile compared to past activity. Skills that permit business owners to successfully manage the enterprise enable them to predict the near-term future, including how high a peak will be, when it will arrive and how long it will last. If the business is offered after the peak is reached, the trend starts to flatten and isn't as positive. Value declines.

When the trend of business is positive, buyers are more attracted and optimistic. They expect the peak to be farther away than it actually may be. As a result, they are more motivated to act, they will extend themselves a little further, and their offers are a little sweeter.

Measured Responses to Create A Productive Sales Environment

Informed buyers build a strong case to support their opinions of business value. They will attempt to get sellers to justify a price. A different set of issues creates anxiety for the novice buyer. He or she can want a lower price without knowing why. In either case, a seller's response sets the tone for continued discussions, if any. It is important to gauge that response, so it is consistent with the situation. Following are a few suggestions for sellers to improve the negotiating environment:

✓ Don't overreact. Keep an open mind, review the conditions and try to understand the buyer's position. Remember, many buyers are inexperienced entrepreneur wanna-be's. They may be representing themselves at the bargaining table. Like sellers, the buyers try to protect themselves; they do this with a very low offer. They might be willing to offer more if they could understand why it is justified. It may be necessary to educate them.

✓ Don't offer a reaction to a first proposal except to listen. The first objective is to understand the specific terms and conditions. Learn what there is to work with.

✓ Go slow. Never hesitate to "sleep" on a proposal. This is a reasonable request. A few hours can produce remarkable changes to an initial perspective. First impressions are helpful – but the details can often change a first impression. Aggressive expiration dates with an offer are a buyer's attempt to take control of the situation. Ignore them if they are unreasonable.

✓ Never Give Something for Nothing. Put buyers on notice early that everything they want comes for a price. It begins

166

with a request for information. Request a Non-Disclosure Agreement first to see if they are serious. Requests for free training might be countered with a higher interest rate if financing is offered. Remember, buyers will only stop asking for more when they discover they have to pay a price.

✓ Convert opinions to offers. Any buyer interested enough to challenge an asking price is usually an interested buyer. He or she might ask small questions to see how much a seller is willing to negotiate. Shrewd buyers often make verbal offers to test the seller's confidence in price. Here is a word to the wise: "Verbal offers are not worth the paper they aren't written on."

✓ Under most conditions a buyer is not obligated to honor a verbal offer. In the give-and-take of negotiating, by responding to a verbal offer, the seller indicates a willingness to negotiate and gets little in return. Treat verbal advances as an opportunity to encourage a written offer.

Effective Phrase

"Entrepreneurs work 16 hours a day for themselves to avoid working eight hours a day for someone else."

The rewards of business ownership are more than money. Sell the business lifestyle. Remind the buyers why they want to buy. They want to work for themselves. They want to be in charge of their days and their destiny. They want to have their own business investment. They want to build wealth. Illustrate this by giving examples of how these benefits are things you get to enjoy by owning the business you are selling to them. Emphasize favorable business trends. Don't delve too far into specifics or how the price is calculated.

A simple response to a verbal offer testing the business price or terms is to inquire whether buyers are willing to put it in writing. If they are, wait until they do. In other cases buyers may attempt to negotiate peripheral issues verbally, too. To these sellers may encourage their further discussion when negotiations captures in writing. It's an easy way to say, "I'm open but uncommitted until you are." The act of putting things in writing can strengthen buyers' resolve and commitment to perform.

Each small piece of information given to a buyer may mean little if considered separately. Together they build a compelling case to support value and contribute to an overall sense of urgency to buy.

15

Plan Ahead to Sell High

> **"When selling yourself don't place too much faith in the three P's."**
>
> 1. Put up a sign.
> 2. Place and ad.
> 3. Pray

When a legitimate buyer shows interest, nothing is more impressive than sellers with all the facts at their fingertips. Business owners are equally empowered when prepared to act quickly.

Assemble Documentation

There are many documents that can be prepared well in advance of a sale. These include but are not limited to the following:

- ✓ The company business plan (current year)
- ✓ The company marketing plan (if written)
- ✓ Corporate resolutions to list and sell the property
- ✓ Certificates of good standing for a corporation
- ✓ Descriptions of all personal property
- ✓ Fictitious name registration
- ✓ Descriptions of real estate with legal description or a lease
- ✓ Negotiated options to extend the real estate lease

✓ Good photographs taken on a clear sunny day

✓ A blank note, security agreement and mortgage or deed

✓ A check list of things to do after a buy/sell agreement is accepted

✓ Request forms for credit references and a buyer's personal financial statement

✓ A blank bill of sale

✓ A title report on the real estate (showing it is marketable)

✓ A current franchise operating circular and agreement (if applicable)

✓ Competitive market analysis or intelligence

✓ A list of vendors and key contacts

✓ A customer list

✓ Samples of marketing materials, advertisements, and press clippings, etc.

These and other forms and documents will permit a seller to act as fast as a buyer.

Ensuring a fictitious name registration is in place may seem excessive. It is not. Buyers have been known, in the absence of such a document, to register the existing business name in their own name. Their next move is to approach the owner with a demand they cease using their existing business name because it is not their property, or lower the asking price. Imagine such a prospect, and the negotiating power it could create. Don't let it happen - plan ahead.

These preparations are part of an overall strategy that gives a buyer no reason to say "no." When the time comes, this advance preparation will help a seller stay focused on running the business while negotiating its sale. Maintaining a calm, confident and organized state of mind at that time is sure to be perceived as strength.

Explain & Prove Performance

Anticipate a qualified buyer's request for financial documentation to justify the asking price. Any attempt to finance the purchase price [at a bank] will automatically trigger a request for three to five years of business financial statements and tax returns. What if the buyer doesn't understand the difference between net profit and cash flow? To be safe, along with financial statements, build an ERCON (earnings reconstruction) for the past three to five years, too. For each of these years illustrate the difference between net profit and cash flow. From this it is possible to show trends in trailing revenue, costs and earnings.

Key Information

The biggest mistake sellers can make: Overprice their property. Some may think it's under-priced and taking a hit. When the property is under-priced it usually sells. The seller receives something. When overpriced, it doesn't sell quickly - maybe never sells. As a result the property languishes on the market for years, perhaps, and then can be liquidated. This produces nothing for goodwill that earlier might have justified a reasonable value.

Consider a Buyer's Need for Income

It is also a good idea to estimate management compensation since this has an effect on business value (and is used in all valuation methods). Complement that information with input from local sources. Consider keeping this information private, however, since buyers may be willing to pay a lower level of compensation than a departing seller who's had it all to him or herself.

Forecasting

Predicting business results that are yet to come is a difficult thing to do. The best advice is, "don't." If a business is sold "proforma," or as if it were to produce certain results and it doesn't, a buyer is sure to be dissatisfied. Buyer's remorse is powerful. It is better to let buyers do their own forecasting.

Alternatively, in the presence of a strong business trend selling from a forecast might be justifiable. In addition to the ERCON, it is possible to construct a one-year forecast of revenue, net profit and cash flow. The company accountant can help. This forecast needs to be as accurate as possible. The success of buyers financed by a seller will depend on the quality of the forecast. The goal is to try to identify business "momentum."

For purposes of valuing the business to sell, however, the following are realistic approaches to consider. Business momentum, using trends and a forecast, can be used to build a value range. This is like a buyer's value range but with a small difference. A seller's value range uses business market values created from the current year and a forecast of next year's financial results. Assuming business is increasing, take the average of values calculated from these results (this year's value and next year's value). This becomes an asking price.

Alternatively, if the business is not cyclical but trending up, one might forecast the next twelve months of results from the month most recently completed. Either approach keeps the seller from over-pricing the business.

Effective Phrase

"People should be less concerned with the difference between good or bad and right or wrong and more concerned with sense and nonsense."

Carl Jung

The wisdom of this phrase is evident. It suggests a business doesn't always grow and prosper by limiting itself to strategies that are tried and true. Some of the best solutions may be the most unorthodox. Those who move in the opposite direction of conventional wisdom can create fortunes. But even these unconventional movers and shakers have a logical basis to support their ideas. Those with the skill to make a sensible argument to support their positions are valuable planners and forecasters. Always form a logical premise for decisions made and used to construct a business forecast or plan. That way, whether right or wrong, you always have a reason for positions you take. This makes you valuable. When you don't have a plan, others that need them don't need you.

This tactic raises the price, though not so high as to be considered excessive. Buyers will determine for themselves if the asking price is "about to be" justified. Caution: When forecasting earnings, keep these private – marked "not for distribution." When appropriate, give buyers enough information to prepare their own forecasts. Trailing results and basic trend analysis of historical results is sufficient. Otherwise a seller's forecast of future results can be interpreted as a promise of what is to come. There are no guarantees.

Target Buyers Pay Most

Two types of buyers exist for a business. The best sales strategy to attract one or the other is to identify which can derive the most benefits from the business offered. Because they have different objectives, this should be taken into consideration when deciding the right benefits to emphasize.

The most frequently encountered small business buyers will be owner/operators. They are interested in buying a business and operating it personally. They want employment income and the ability to service acquisition debt until paid under reasonable conditions. A marketing effort to attract this buyer should emphasize these benefits. It will also paint a picture of the creative fulfillment available from ownership, since this is a co-benefit of some importance – the sizzle of the steak. Remember, this buyer wants to become free if currently employed. Show the buyer how buying this business can make it so.

The second, less common buyer is an investor or financial buyer. This buyer is making a business investment and does not want to run the business. This may be a practicing entrepreneur, or a larger business on the prowl for good acquisitions. Either seeks growth by non-organic means – to buy instead of build. To them the creative fulfillment of business ownership is less important; financial results are the priority. Recall, the owner/operator wants employment income – management compensation will be an important issue alongside free cash flow to service debt. Investors will be concerned about these points too, but the acquisition is less personal. These buyers normally hire someone else to manage the business. Also, most investors are looking for opportunities that offer synergy.

The ability to reduce the costs of management compensation, administration, marketing and production can have a dramatic improvement on net profit. Moreover, these types of buyers often have more cash and may not need financing. Therefore, free cash flow is measured as a return on investment of cash. As a result, price may be a function of the capitalization rate selected. Investors are more aggressive and select high cap rates. The acceptable asking price can go up when synergy is present. If synergy is added to build cash flow, savings occur and improve free cash flow. This can be estimated. The business value can increase because the benefits justify more. For example, suppose synergy creates a savings of $20,000 to a particular investor using an 18% cap rate to value business investments. The indicated value is $221,844. This compares very favorably to the market value of approximately $185,000 for BELL-Quest, Ltd., the example company. Does it include more goodwill? Absolutely. But it is very saleable. Investors recognize the value of intellectual capital. When the numbers fit they are more willing to act.

Sellers need to decide early which buyer is most likely to be attracted to their offering. The defining criterion is, surprisingly, not always good financial results. Investors seeking to grow by acquiring more of what they already have may pay a reasonable price. More is paid for acquisitions with synergy and unique, productive intellectual capital. With a few price comparisons, it is possible to target the right buyer.

Make a note: While investors may sometimes pay more, they can be harder to find and tougher to sell. A business must have a high cash flow to successfully attract a premium from them. In most cases, the small business opportunity with fewer than 10 employees is best suited to meet the needs of an owner or operator.

16

Business "Sale By Owner" Strategies

"Don't give buyers a reason to say 'No'."

Selling a business without the assistance of a brokerage professional can be an effective strategy. This is commonly called a "For Sale By Owner" approach. Most who choose this method of sale wish to avoid paying what they perceive to be a large brokerage commission. They believe they know their business well enough to sell it themselves and, they think they have the ability to advertise their business "confidentially" to keep their intentions a secret. All of this is plausible, but not as easy as it sounds.

Business brokerage commissions of 10% are common - it can cost thousands to sell a business. Those who choose "Sale By Owner" might expect to get the job done for less. It is possible, however, a support team is required to help sell a business - and they don't work for free.

Another misconception is that sellers know their business better than anyone who may attempt to sell it for them. This is a misguided assumption. Most sellers know how to sell their goods and services to make a business profit. Selling the entire business, however, is a very different kind of "goods or service" and requires a different type of skill, which most sellers don't possess. This phenomenon is often discovered too late by those attempting to franchise their business. Running a business that sells and serves franchises is not the same as operating a franchise.

Finally, sellers know how to attract buyers to their business to buy what they sell. Attracting buyers to buy the entire business requires a different approach. Many sellers are not well schooled in how to attract buyers, confidentially, to buy a business.

Still, many business owners sell their own businesses. Those who succeed usually have a good plan of action to follow. This helps keep the business sales process from becoming a distraction to running the business. Unfocused effort produces poor results. Sellers who want to sell their own business should begin by remembering three things every seller really wants.

The Highest Price

A business's highest price is the value buyers are ready, willing and able to pay – today. The highest price is a recognizable value. It is easily justified, offers reasonable management compensation and can support acquisition financing required. The highest price attracts lots of buyers. Try to imagine how much easier it is to negotiate potentially lucrative finer points of one offer when three other offers are in play. The old rule is, "While you're writing offers in the stock room keep talking with buyers in the conference room."

Knowing a business's highest price is a more important issue to sellers planning to market the business themselves. They don't have time to speculate; their time is limited. While a business is on the market, the owner's interest costs (if any) and other related direct and indirect holding costs continue. These can have an unfavorable impact on business performance and sale price. So the highest price is joined at the hip to the time it takes to sell a business.

The Shortest Time

When most entrepreneurs decide to sell, they want it to happen yesterday. This is because a new business vision, inconsistent with current conditions, may already be in place in their minds. Under these conditions, ownership's focus is distracted and management effectiveness is often diminished. This is a bad combination of events and can be costly. Standards of performance decline, and new opportunities are missed. The entrepreneurial spirit that drove the company to success is diminished. Burnout can easily occur.

When a property is available for a long time (more than six months), the owner can also become frustrated with the sales process. This is natural and easier to deal with when one knows what to expect. Frustration is greater if ownership's intent to sell does not remain confidential. Employees are not blind. Learning the boss is selling out may encourage them to consider employment elsewhere. Employee turnover has significant direct and indirect costs. New employees must be found and trained before becoming productive – another distraction. Customers learning of the business sale may notice changes, too, and take their business elsewhere. When attempting to sell, the timing of these reactions could not be worse.

The combination of factors described can negatively affect revenue, expenses, net profit, cash flow and the business value. Worse, intelligent buyers who notice a business languishing on the market will take longer to act, hoping the price will fall farther. Clearly, the situation can be grim for the unprepared. There is, however, a solution.

Working behind the scenes, sellers can anticipate and develop a complete business disposition strategy. It takes six months, a year or perhaps even two to maximize the results, but it can be worth the effort.

The Least Effort

Face it. Selling a business is not always easy. It is unwise to assume the one-in-a-million buyers with money to burn will magically appear. It is better to prepare for a well-informed buyer. Also, don't be too focused on finding a buyer that wants to own and operate the specific type of business you offer. Small business buyers will generally entertain a variety of small business types provided they represent a good investment value. This should help widen the pool of buyers that can be attracted and increase the chances a sale will occur. With a good preparation to sell the sales process can be set in motion. Selling your business can be accomplished with a series of small incremental steps taken over time that considerably reduce the effort expended. This strategy works best.

Time on the market is correlated to preparation. When a business offering is well planned and available at a reasonable price, a sale occurs much faster. That is because capable buyers know a good deal when they see one. They also know it won't last. Good sales plans and pricing strategies engage a buyer's sense of urgency to act. Building a sense of urgency among buyers makes the seller's job easier.

To begin a Sale By Owner process, create a detailed plan of action — a sales plan. Successful sellers do their thinking early to ensure better execution later. Here are seven strategies of successful business sales plans. It goes without saying that all are preceded by the important task of creating a well-justified business value.

Sales Strategy #1:
Assemble and Use a Support Team

Many attempting to sell their own businesses ask whether or not they should engage others to help them and, if so, how much they should pay. Selling your own business is a team effort and often includes the business accountant, attorney, an advertising professional and, in some cases, a broker. Each can play a meaningful position on the team, but the seller must assume responsibility as its captain. Make contact with each team member before you begin.

√ **Accountants** - A good accountant can help organize and prepare financial information that will be meaningful to buyers. Most already understand how a business is valued and can confirm the work performed by a seller. This can save lots of money. Accountants can also provide statistics about similar businesses to support investment value. Also, buyer confidence in a business opportunity grows when buyers inspect financial records printed on an accountant's stationery.

√ **Lawyers** - These professionals fulfill the valuable function of translating agreements into writing. This will include non-disclosure agreements, letters of intent, offers to purchase, and all closing documents. They have escrow accounts that can be used to hold deposits and sales proceeds. This is all a necessity. Lawyers also have the secret handshake that is often required.

It is common for buyers to engage the services of an attorney to represent them in a transaction. It's the smart thing to do. It is unwise for a seller to attempt negotiating directly with an attorney; retaining a lawyer to stand in for the seller improves negotiations. Lawyers can talk to each other, get things done, and move the sales process forward.

√ **Advertising & Public Relations Professionals** - Advertising professionals can help plan a campaign to advertise the business. Their copywriting experience enables them to write energetic advertising that will attract buyers. Knowledge of the industry gives them the ability to recommend newspapers and alternative publications where effective advertising can be placed. They know the goal of advertising is to generate leads, not sell the business. Using their skill will accomplish this important objective.

Public Relations experts can plan, write and release press releases about a business to local media. They can position business owners as local experts on pertinent topics and important news sources. This strategy raises the profile of the business. If local buyers exist, this may attract their attention without the exposure of local advertising.

√ **Brokers** - The goal of selling a business directly to save a brokerage commission doesn't mean a broker couldn't act as part of a team. Brokers are a valuable resource. Utilizing them as consultants paid by the hour can be very helpful. It is an option every business owner should seriously consider. They may offer benefits that outweigh the cost.

Brokers already know the market, and competent ones can quickly evaluate the desirability of a business opportunity. They can make objective recommendations to improve the process and the result. For a flat fee or an hourly rate they can meet regularly with sellers to ensure they are staying with the plan. Plus, if results are not achieved brokers can become "Plan B." Brokers already may have created many marketing mechanisms needed to promote the sale of a business. They may be linked with qualified buyers waiting for a good opportunity. In such cases it could be less costly to pay their commission than to proceed alone. Under the right conditions using a broker can be a real savings of time and money.

Use the Bluebook Appendix

Refer to the section titled "General Terms and Features of an Acquisition" for more information on the sales process. This section includes helpful explanations of key issues, conveniently arranged alphabetically.

Selling Strategy#2:
Early to Bed, Early to Rise,
Work Like Hell and ADVERTISE

Every seller wants to advertise his or her business to every buyer on the planet while keeping it a secret. That's not possible. Nevertheless, any plan to successfully sell a business will involve some form of advertising. It is possible to let the word out in ways that do not disturb the confidentiality sellers crave. Effective advertising in other geographic markets often accomplishes this feat.

Very often the best buyers for a business are not local. This will be particularly the case in rural areas. Local (in this case rural or suburban) investors' historical bias disqualifies them. The local buyer remembers when the business offered was started or purchased years earlier for much less, inhibiting the ability to think in terms of current-day values. Also, local investors already are located in the market; moving to a new location is not a motivating factor.

Out-of-area buyers don't have the historical bias. They want to relocate. This is especially true of those attempting to move from the city to the country. In an environment where jobs are scarce by comparison, buying a business in a small town is a powerful lure. Properties a local buyer wouldn't take on a bet could be a city buyer's dream come true.

Effective advertising would include placements in classified sections of newspapers serving regional metropolitan areas. Target those areas that seem to be the former homes of local residents. This rule of thumb also is a practical way to select a city in which to advertise your business. "Buyers often move from North to South and East to West." That's because business buyers are far enough along in their careers to be looking for a better climate, less congestion and a simpler existence.

Blind advertisements are those that describe the business without revealing its identity. Use descriptive phrases like, "Low Stress Lifestyle" to make a business sell like bacon smells. Give basic information only and set up a post office box to receive inquiries. Many newspapers can provide this service for a small fee.

Selling Strategy #3:
Qualify the Buyer

A well-qualified buyer can perform. The capabilities of a buyer that has not been qualified are questionable. It takes a great deal of time to sell a business; don't waste it on buyers that can't perform. The quickest way to qualify a buyer is by asking them to sign a Non-Disclosure Agreement early. Buyers who are serious, motivated, well-informed and capable will understand the need for this. They have nothing to hide if the request for the non-disclosure is linked to an additional request for "like-kind" financial information such as a financial statement at a later date. Unqualified buyers will balk at these requests. Also, determine the buyer's objectives. It will be helpful to remind them of these as the negotiations continue. Determine their investment criteria to help create a fit between them and the business. Until there is a fit, it is unlikely a sale will occur.

Key Information

Buyers Are Expensive.

It can cost hundreds, even thousands, of dollars in time an effort to attract a buyer ready, willing and able to buy a business. When buyers surface, don't let them get away. It costs more to find a new buyer than to keep working with one already on the scene. The key to keeping a buyer interested - and making efficient use of advertising dollars and ownership's time - is to qualify them accurately. Use this information to avoid giving them a reason to say "No" to acquiring the business.

Qualifying a buyer is a specific skill that often takes years to learn. But you can learn it quickly by taking a simple approach. Just attempt to get to know the buyer before attempting to sell them your business. It is essentially a chemical test to see if the principals' values mix well or create sparks. Without good chemistry and shared values it is unlikely a sale can be negotiated. One good way to test for buyer and seller chemistry is with a phone call between principals. Another is a simple meeting during breakfast or lunch in a public restaurant. Both of these venues provide a neutral environment.

When qualifying a buyer, pay less attention to what they want and more to what they need. This is important because buyers ALWAYS want to talk about and focus on things they want from a business and NEVER use these as a basis for investment. Sellers must be shrewd enough to distinguish a buyer's wants from their needs. The qualifying process is the time to determine what they are and which is which. The decision to buy is nearly always based on the latter - NEEDS.

For example, a buyer who needs $50,000 of management compensation from a business to support his family may go on and on about the nifty product line or location of your business. They may speak endlessly about being their own boss for a change, as well. But they will not buy a business that has everything they want if it doesn't have enough compensation to meet their income needs.

Don't be afraid to ask these and other questions. Qualifying a buyer can save a lot of time working with people unable to perform. It can also help tailor a transaction to suit the buyer's needs. Keep the discussions rolling by accentuating the positive and deferring discussion of potential deal breakers while successfully negotiating smaller issues.

Effective Phrase

Qualifying Questions You'll Want to Ask a Buyer

1. Why do you want to buy a business, this business?
2. Do your spouse and family support business ownership?
3. What sort of work do you do now and have you done in the past?
4. Are you buying for yourself or another, and do you have any partners?
5. How much annual income are you accustomed to earning?
6. How much equity - cash - do you have available, today, to invest in a business you want to buy?
7. Will you need financing?
8. What interests you about my business?
9. What are some other objectives you want to accomplish by acquiring your own business?
10. If you find a business that meets your criteria, today, are you prepared to take action now and buy it?

Selling Strategy #4:
Give Buyers What They Want

The typical buyer profile is a person who wants to buy a business and become self-employed so they can escape from a dead-end job. They want the business to offer reasonable financial leverage with a modest down payment. Business cash flow should be sufficient to pay off the acquisition debt in a reasonable amount of time. Don't let your ego take control and suggest it takes a degree in rocket science to successfully operate your business. Make it seem simple. In summary, the business should be easy to buy, easy to pay for, and easy to run. Structuring the sale of a business with a price, terms and benefits that accomplish these objectives provides a much greater chance of selling.

Selling Strategy #5:
Do Things For Buyers
They Cannot Do For Themselves

This is the first rule of successful selling. When executed it makes a seller more valuable to a buyer. That makes it easier to lead a buyer through the sales process.

> "Milton Erickson was a famous psychologist who treated patients using the power of a paradox. He learned his craft early on the family farm. One day he was observing his father attempting to pull their bull out of the barn. No matter how hard he pulled on the rope around the bull's neck, the animal only resisted more and moved backwards. Young Milton asked his father if he might try to move the bull. He began taking the rope and gently walking around the bull, turning him so he was facing into the barn. Then, he pulled on the rope with all his strength and the bull backed out of the barn. The moral of the story is, "You can manipulate me all you want just so long as I like it."

Typically, when attempting to buy a business there are three things most buyers cannot do for themselves. These are: 1) justify the business value, 2) secure financing and, 3) take the next step. Justifying business value is easy to do if the business is properly priced. One only needs to know the buyer's basic income needs to illustrate how the business earning power can meet them. Securing financing is easy if a seller wishes to finance the sale. If sellers want cash, a well-justified price will also make it easier for a buyer to secure financing from a bank. The third is a result of inexperience that, typically, is not a problem for sellers. Help buyers take the next step by leading them through the acquisition process. This helps secure their confidence and trust. Both are required before they will write a big check to buy a business.

Selling Strategy #6:
Control the Flow of Information

Generally buyers want to know everything about a business without offering anything, such as an offer, in return. It's called a "free look," something sellers should avoid. Give buyers enough information to create added interest and develop the lead. The objective is to "keep the mystery alive" so it is possible to keep giving buyers more of what they want.

The basic structure of a business sale will involve receipt of a valid, enforceable Non-Disclosure Agreement from buyer to seller. This occurs very early and before any "substantial" information about a business is shared. Next, the buyer is given access to limited information about the business (not financial statements but a summary of business results). Also, the buyer is granted access to a one-on-one with the seller to discuss the details of a business.

After disclosures have been made if the parties agree to proceed a formal offer to purchase should be prepared. Once executed buyers may conduct a thorough due-diligence to verify what they have already learned. Upon completion of this process and satisfaction of any contract contingencies the parties proceed to close.

Use the "evidence room" approach to distribute key information. Once a buyer has indicated sufficient interest to pursue an acquisition, and signed a non-disclosure agreement, set up a meeting between principals. At this meeting the seller should bring confidential summaries of business results, business operations, etc. The buyers might also bring their financial statements. At this meeting each is free to question the other about matters of importance to an acquisition. They can inspect documents brought to the meeting. They may not copy them. At the end of this meeting all parties take with them everything they brought. Thus, the information is only available for inspection in "the evidence room." Using this approach helps parties to a transaction get to know one another better without unnecessary exposure to either.

Selling Strategy #6:
Avoid Distractions

Selling a business while running it can be a major distraction. The reason is running the business might have become boring while selling is charged with new excitement. Those who sell their own businesses must keep their eyes on the ball - maintain revenues and profits so they don't decline. If that happens, the desirability of the business will fall. Here are three especially nasty distractions to avoid.

√ **Burnout** - Many successful careers have ended in burnout when all that was needed was a week off. If burnout is a problem, take time off to get a fresh perspective. It may seem like a costly thing to do, but the price can be small compared to allowing revenue decreases that result in a substantial reduction in business value.

√ **Siren's Song** - Some buyers, especially those from a larger company, may show interest in acquiring the business. An inquiry from a source such as this can easily engage the ego. It can be a destructive path to follow.

Larger businesses often grow by acquisition and, thus, are very experienced. They know the first step is to get the seller's ego engaged. Their initial inquiry often proposes to give the seller "everything they want." There is great danger here. Sellers can spend so much time and energy working with their "big buyer" that they forget to tend to their own business. Buyers detecting this trend slow down, start taking away small things they originally proposed and allow business revenues to decline. The original business value, now more difficult to justify, becomes less. Very frequently a formal offer is finally submitted that is far less than the original "intentions" expressed. The seller is now stuck with the options of selling for less, starting over with another buyer (also at a lower price), or rebuilding a business they are attempting to sell.

Straw Parties. Many buyers - and this is especially true of a competitor - will use a "straw-party" to advance their interest to buy a business. This is a person that has no apparent connection to the real buyer behind the scenes. This is done for two basic reasons.

First, a large company with considerable financial resources doesn't want to reveal its interest. The concern is that sellers realizing this interest will "raise the price." Hence, they attempt to work in secret. A Non-Disclosure Agreement is often sufficient to prevent this problem.

Second, some competitors simply want to learn all they can about the business with no intention to buy. This is an attempt to "pick someone's pockets" for free. It can be very damaging, too. After the buyer inquiry fades, rumors can be released that the business is for sale. This can unfavorably affect business revenue and cause employees to become concerned. With the use of a properly worded Non-Disclosure Agreement this situation also can also be avoided.

17 Tactics to Boost Business Value

**"Remember after working successfully
to increase business value
the original objective was to sell."**

When buying or starting a new business, selling should be the last subject on one's mind, right? Wrong. It should actually be the first. That's because one wants to make the business worth as much as possible. Build value starting on day one; don't wait until you want out. When you know the factors, or variables, that most affect value, you can make profitable decisions from the start – and you'll get the highest possible price when the time comes to sell.

Well that's just great, you may be thinking. I've been in business for years . . . is it too late for me to ensure getting a good price when it's time to sell? Relax. It has been shown it does take a little time to get in a position to sell profitably. Normally, you'll need a year to prepare before putting your company on the market. That way you'll have time to take some tangible steps and make your business more attractive to potential buyers.

As discussed earlier, selling out is supported by a good sales strategy. It gives buyers a sense of urgency to take action and make an offer on what appears to be a great deal. Here are specific tactics that help business value and help motivate buyers to act.

Tactic One:
Location, Location, Location

Secure the business location because it facilitates customer traffic that leads to sales, profit and, ultimately, higher business value. Develop assurances the location won't change after the sale occurs. Here's how:

If the property is leased, renegotiate the terms with options to renew. This will provide added security for the potential buyer.

If you own the real estate occupied by your business, consider refinancing it to withdraw your equity. Increasing your cash reserves will be helpful during the selling process and, if the buyer wants to acquire the real estate too, the financing is already in place.

Tactic Two:
Develop an Internet Presence

This is a second business location on the World Wide Web. It can bring more traffic to your business and has promotional value. A website can increase revenues during the year before a business is offered for sale. And higher revenues translate into a higher selling price. A proactively-managed Web site also creates the impression you are "in the game."

Tactic Three:
Create Curb Appeal

Dogs don't sell very well. A business that looks like a dog tells a buyer there's lots of deferred maintenance to be performed. That will take cash that might otherwise be used to buy the business.

Clean up and fix up your business before you make it available for sale. Make it shine, both fiscally and physically, by selling off dated inventory, attending to repairs or equipment needs, and releasing nonessential personnel and replacing them by outsourcing, if possible. Then when a buyer comes calling there's little to do other than take over. The amount they can invest and your business value can be greater.

Tactic Four:
Reduce Uncertainty

Most sellers are afraid to tell employees they will be selling the business because of unfavorable reactions and early departures. You can reduce this uncertainty by periodically reminding staff that every business asset owned is for sale every day you own it. Prepare yourself to make financial disclosures a buyer will want. Have your accountant build a business cash flow analysis. Don't give buyers a reason to say no. Nolo Supre Prendre - Eliminate surprises.

Tactic Five:
Stop Skimming

An old saying goes, "The difference between tax evasion and tax avoidance is five to ten years in jail." Skimming happens when a business owner receives income but does not report it for income tax purposes. Skimming is tax evasion and it is illegal. Plus, it reduces the business income, profit and value. If you skim, stop. You'll eliminate tax and legal entanglements, and the bottom line and business value will improve. Remember, "skimming is that portion of the business price you take before you put the business up for sale."

Tactic Six:
Build a Succession Plan

A buyer may be unsure of his or her ability to run your business after the sale. You can assure him or her by offering a training program, which includes a timetable to explain the basics of how your business works and a plan for the seller's involvement, which should gradually cease, usually within about 60 days.

Tactic Seven:
Become More Visible

There are two times to increase the business advertising budget in business. One is when business is terrible and your competitors can't afford the cost. Then you can increase market share at their expense. The other is when you plan to sell out. More advertising prior to a sale of the business increases the public's awareness of your business. It's a subtle way to attract a buyer's attention. This is important because someone in your marketplace is likely to be your buyer. The more they see your name, the greater their perception of your presence in the market place. That increases their perception of your business's value.

A strong public relations effort will further compliment the effort to build the image of your business prior to a sale. Become a local expert for your industry. Do this by presenting valuable information to your community via press releases, talks or visits with local clubs. Offer your knowledge as a news source to area media outlets. Try to find a news story from your industry that would be of interest to their audience. People trust the industry experts. Trust builds business value.

Tactic Eight:
Eliminate Weaknesses

Prepare a brief summary or an extensive review of your business. Either way, it must be done in preparation for a sale. You can hire a business valuation analyst or do it yourself, with step-by-step guidance from this book. Perform your own due diligence. Develop your own pricing multiple in the process. From this exercise you will identify the strengths and weaknesses of your business. Restaurant operators might focus their attention on ways to lower food costs to increase gross profit. Manufacturers that eliminate deferred maintenance by refurbishing equipment enable buyer's to commit more cash available to buying their business. Retailers can sell off dated inventory for a modest discount instead of selling it for cost or less when included in a sale of the business. These tactics eliminate a business's weaknesses and build its strengths thereby creating a more desirable, secure investment opportunity.

Tactic Nine:
Identify Synergy

All buyers want to find synergies in businesses they buy. Synergy has a favorable impact on business results. It makes the business investment more attractive. When synergy exists the business price can be higher than when it does not and must be developed. Recognizing the types of synergy your business has will enable you to target a specific category of buyers who will pay the highest price.

Buyers who want to run a business look for situations where they can use their skills. For example, if you are selling a retail business, don't think about selling it to a person retiring from a manufacturing job. They like being left alone and would have little interest. This is important to remember if financing the sale. Such a person could quickly develop distaste for customers and acquire a personality like sandpaper. The business will not fare very well under their ownership. Collecting on your note could become questionable. Sell instead to people familiar with sales professions. Leveraging existing knowledge to run a business reduces the learning curve. A shorter learning curve leads to improved performance and results. Identify the critical types of work a buyer must perform to successfully run your business. Then try to identify a source of buyers that would possess these skills. They will be more attracted to the business and pay a higher price.

Investors - financial buyers - buy businesses for raw earning power. They want a return on their money. Frequently, they own other businesses and their motive is to combine the costs of certain expenses such as accounting, legal, advertising, procurement, location, shipping, etc. This is the type of synergy they often seek. In many cases they buy businesses to increase the buying power of several businesses. Purchasing in larger quantities often results in greater quantity discounts. The retained price, however, may remain unchanged. The difference saved is added profit. Some of this difference can be used to justify a bigger business value.

Tactic Ten:
Structure More Than One Transaction Option

Develop alternative sales options so your business can appeal to a larger array of buyers. For example, sell for cash or finance the property yourself. Sell the business and keep your business real estate – lease it to the business buyer. Or, sell the business and place the real estate into an IRC 1031 Tax-Deferred Exchange. Various selling options will create the flexibility needed to accommodate the investment capabilities of a larger number of buyers. The odds of selling increase.

Regardless of the option you select, remember to qualify the business and the buyer. Qualify the business by selecting a pricing strategy that makes financial sense to a buyer. No buyer can succeed who buys a business priced so high the chances of making a profit are virtually eliminated. With a realistic price it is possible to offer seller financing or sell for cash. Then qualify the buyer to ensure they have the financial capability and professional skill to run the business successfully. Remember, a qualified buyer can pay more.

Tactic Eleven:
Cash in Your Good Will

Service businesses — professional and labor-intensive — can carry an impressive value and they can be sold. There are specific ways owners can up the ante on their asking price.

For example, many think it is not possible to sell a consultancy, catering business or window-washing service. Even if you don't have anything tangible to sell such as inventory, equipment or even real estate, it doesn't matter. You can still place a real value on your enterprise. Most entrepreneurs, *especially* in the service industry, have no idea what their business is worth. Unfortunately, neither do buyers so, with this level of uncertainty, chances are they won't pay much.

> **"**Many ask how to value a service business.
> That's the wrong question. They should ask
> how to give a service business value.**"**

The most important tactic to recovering goodwill in a sales price is to give the service business more value. Create this value by recognizing that the intangible assets — also called intellectual capital or, more commonly, goodwill —

make a worthwhile contribution to business performance. Intangible assets are your reputation in the community, the knowledge of how your business is run, your secret recipes, your skilled staff - the list goes on. The challenge is converting these intangibles into tangible assets a buyer will want to acquire. Rise to the challenge by making these assets part of the business – institutionalize them. That way when you leave the business, revenue doesn't walk out the door with you. Here are some easy tactics to consider.

√ **Convert client lists into contracts** - Which is worth more: a business with 200 client names or one with 200 client contracts? You may have a steady flow of customers and those that return often, but neither you nor a buyer can accurately assess the future revenue in a service business. Change that by offering clients a 5 percent discount to sign a contract for a year with a 30-day exit clause. They have little to lose and you have much to gain: more committed customers and a greater perception of business value. It's a smart business decision to insure income and will make your business far more appealing to buyers.

√ **Adjust pricing** - Small service companies usually have lower operating costs than larger businesses, so they often price their services for less. Contracts that create a backlog of business are of little value if the billing rates are so low the potential buyer couldn't make a profit. Raise prices to match the competition (who might be buyers for your business).

√ **Transfer your knowledge** - Accept the reality that you can be replaced. Sometimes our strengths become our weaknesses in that maybe you do know how best to serve your clients, but what happens if you're sick or overloaded with work? Get other people involved in your duties by teaching them how to do your job. Then when you, the owner, leave the business upon sale, the enterprise won't fall apart. This is the kind of assurance potential suitors want and need to have.

√ **Pump up your marketing and exposure strategy** - Today, many people think they can slap a web site together and the world will come calling. In fact, web sites do attract inquiries and they facilitate administrative functions. Yet they have zero value if you don't promote them. Advertise web sites in newspapers, magazines, on your letterhead and business cards, or any other place your audience might notice to help drive more business to the site and, ultimately, to increase your revenues.

√ **Reduce employee turnover** - If your business centers around the services you or your employees perform for clients, make sure those employees — the ones you've spent lots of time training — stick around by:

✓ instituting programs that encourage them to stay, such as retirement with long-term vesting;

✓ paying your people well and giving them bonuses;

✓ creating a culture that is inviting and makes people bang down the door to come to work; and

✓ treating employees like entrepreneurs.

All of these steps will encourage a low turnover rate, making your business more profitable and stable — which is appealing to potential buyers.

√ **Document and copyright your work** - Training employees can be complex and time-consuming. It usually helps to have some sort of outline. Turn that information — which is how your business is run — into a manual so a buyer can take over with ease. Now you'll have something tangible when offering to sell the business. This sort of documentation of how your business runs is the way franchises begin. Franchisers are masters at documented processes, but everyone, even Mom and Pop shops, can and should do this.

√ **Be prepared to defend** - It's easy to copy some businesses. If the heart of your service business is "intellectual capital," then protect it. to prove you were there first, start by documenting who, what, where, when and how. Use service marks and trademarks. Copyright your materials. All of these steps are necessary if you ever need to defend your stake. By doing so, you also will be able to better assess and value your enterprise for potential sale or just to improve the way you run the business.

Take these steps to identify and improve the value of service businesses. Then you can approach the bargaining table with low uncertainty and a legitimate, documented measurement of business value — especially for those intangibles. All these tactics are within the grasp of most business owners. You can't put them to work, however, unless you can measure their impact on value. A proper valuation is the lynchpin of any effort to boost business value.

18 Selling the Parts for More

"When separated the business and real estate might bring a greater value."

Ownership of both a business and the real estate it occupies is common among small business entrepreneurs. This arrangement often results in a special situation when it is time to plan an exit strategy. In essence, both properties may be available when it is time to sell out. Ownership frequently attempts to sell them as a package deal for one price. Valuable marketing and income benefits might be realized, however, by offering these properties as separate investments.

The Evolution of Ownership

Typically, entrepreneurs start or buy a small business first. They are driven by a desire to work for themselves at this early stage of entrepreneurship. The business opportunity is the primary target. A different motive is involved when making a commercial real estate investment.

Later, during the evolution of ownership, wealth building and continued business security emerge as dominant issues. Additional business assets are often acquired to support these objectives. Acquiring the real estate occupied by the business is one of the more obvious acquisitions entrepreneurs entertain. This move can build wealth and ensure continued access to a proven business location – a key ingredient of predictable business success. When it is time to sell, however, entrepreneurs are well advised to consider unwinding their business and real estate in stages rather than all at once.

Create a Buyer's Market

When it is time to sell out, business owners want three things: 1) the highest price; 2) in the shortest time; and 3) using the least amount of effort. Offering the business and real estate separately may be the best approach to realize these goals.

When business assets are divided the price for each will be less than the total of the two. A lower business price will attract a larger number of buyers. More important, a greater percentage of these buyers are likely to be qualified to make the investment. As a result, the ability to solicit realistic offers improves and, with it, the strength of the seller's negotiating hand. Chances are good a better price will be received.

Experience shows that with a reasonable marketing effort there is an inverse relationship between the pool of buyers created and the time it takes to sell. More of one means less of the other. As mentioned earlier, when a business and real estate are priced together, the higher price disqualifies thousands of would-be buyers. It takes longer to sell when the supply of buyers is limited. Alternatively, when a business is offered separately from the real estate, for a much lower price, the number of capable buyers grows. It takes less time to sell.

Curiously, many small business owners overlook the hard and soft costs of extended sales effort. They can be substantial and far greater that the difference between a price that is too high and one that is realistic. Many entrepreneurs sell because of burnout. And yet, from this negatively charged state of mind, they are forced to continue operating a business while simultaneously launching a typically covert marketing effort to sell out. If overpriced, the business can languish on the market for more than a year. During this time negative thinking may have an unfavorable impact on revenue and profit. If competitors discover a sale is contemplated they may attempt to bleed off customers so more revenue is lost. Still worse, key employees who learn of an impending sale may become insecure and seek employment elsewhere. Employee turnover costs are often one to two times their annual earnings, so operating costs rise. Burnout, loss of confidentiality, customers and employee turnover all contribute unfavorably to business performance. The final sales price often decreases as the time it takes to sell increases. Selling the business separately helps prevent this unpleasant phenomenon.

Instilling a sense of urgency to act in legitimate buyers is crucial to selling a business. After comparing prices of small businesses, many knowledgeable buyers become adept at recognizing a good value. With the real estate included a business offering may not be as attractive an investment as it might be without the property. This is because businesses typically produce higher returns than commercial real estate. When the enterprise is offered separately its return is not dragged down or diluted by the lesser-performing property. The economics of the business offering are more attractive and will motivate buyers. When a motivated buyer arrives on the scene, less effort is required to negotiate the sale.

Separate the Real Estate and Business Values

Separating a business and its real estate involves both legal and financial considerations. Many times the real estate will be held in a small private corporation that can make the process less complicated. If not, it may be necessary to sell only the business assets and keep the real property. Legal counsel and a tax-advisor should be consulted to help determine the best approach.

The following example will compare and illustrate the impact on financial results when a strategy to sell a business and its real estate separately is applied. Using four common small business valuation techniques, the following range of values is developed.

VALUE RANGE For Combined Value of Business & Real Estate	
Capitalization Method	$173,322
Excess Earnings Method	$190,782
Leveraged Cash Flow (Seller Financed)	$187,292
Leveraged Cash Flow (Bank Financed)	$177,835

Measures of central tendency offer one way to develop a market value from this value range. A simple formula to produce this result follows.

RANGE ANALYSIS To Determine Market Value	
Mean Value	$182,308
Range	$ 17,460
Median of Range	$ 8,730
Low Value in the Range	$173,322
Market Value of Business (Median)	$182,052

The close similarity between the range mean and median or market business value suggests the values estimated are highly accurate.

Calculating the value for the business real estate is not difficult. Local market professionals use comparative market analyses to develop fairly reliable estimates of property value. If desired, qualified real estate appraisers can provide added input to reduce uncertainty. When a [real estate] value is established it can be subtracted from the price for both property and business. Here is a new range of values to illustrate this adjustment. (For this example, assume the real estate has a market value of $105,000)

VALUE RANGE For Business When Real Estate is Subtracted	
Capitalization Method	$ 68,322
Excess Earnings Method	$ 85,782
Leveraged Cash Flow (Seller Financed)	$ 82,292
Leveraged Cash Flow (Bank Financed)	$ 72,835

Using measures of central tendency the market value indicated is $77,052.

Simply subtracting the value of real estate from business value does not, however, address the issue of affordability. How will cash flow be affected by rent to be paid on the building? And how much should that be? These are important concerns that prompt a more detailed approach.

Determining the value of a business from its intrinsic qualities is a little more involved but may yield favorable results. A limited supply of business appraisers makes it more difficult to secure this information. Where available, their services can be quite costly. If the business is small it may not be cost effective either. Business comparable sales are of little help because the number of cases to consider is often too small to be useful. Where a larger sample can be found additional problems may exist. Out of date information, lack of similarity to the subject business, and a remote location of cases in the sampling of comparable sales may prevent the analyst using this approach to accurately extrapolate business value.

Accurate Variables Lead to Reliable Values

Consider determining business value by using a combination of basic valuation formulas. The capitalization, excess earnings and leveraged cash flow techniques are simple yet effective approaches to measuring the value of a small business. Details of these valuation techniques can be found in the Business Valuation Bluebook. Start by assembling a set of variables.

✓ Real Estate Market Value - $105,000;

✓ Inventory @ Cost - $55,000;

✓ Fixtures & Equipment - $5,000 [Market not Book Value];

✓ Cash Flow - $50,432

✓ Safe Rate of Return – 6.00%

✓ Capitalization Rate - 11.5%.

✓ Financing: One valuation method relies on financing to establish business value. Terms are adjusted to be consistent with shorter class life of assets used to secure business acquisition debt.

Next, minor adjustments to the cash flow are necessary. A reasonable rent expense for the property occupied by the business must be included in the business expenses. Sometimes the amount sellers charge themselves [when they also own the real estate] is far below market value. On other occasions rent may be omitted entirely as an operating cost. Now, because the real estate is to be excluded from a sale, rent must be estimated and treated as a business expense. But at what amount?

One way to determine rent is to review rates offered for similar business space per square foot. Then apply this factor to determine the market value of space provided by the business real estate being retained and leased. Another technique to determine property rent for the subject property involves treating the income required on the investment value of the property as rent. Assume a capitalization rate on the building of 9.75%. This is less than a business cap rate because there is less risk involved, however, it is still 1% over a prime interest rate. Next, calculate the ROI indicated from a commercial real estate investment worth $105,000 at the selected capitalization rate. The income should be $10,238. This figure will be treated as rent on the building and applied to the earnings reconstruction as below.

Reconstructed Business Earnings

Using either approach the increased rent expense appears as a negative adjustment in a reconstructed profit and loss statement. This illustrates the variance between business taxable income and cash flow. In cases where the separation of assets occurs, sellers normally offer business buyers a triple-net lease for the real property. The lessee pays all property insurance, taxes, repairs and maintenance. Since these expenses are often included in profit and loss statement it may not be necessary to make an additional adjustment to business cash flow. Adjusting for increased rent reduces cash flow and free cash flow (cash flow less management compensation) by an equal amount.

209

EARNINGS RECONSTRUCTION	
Revenue	$608,951
Cost of Goods	< 397,530>
Gross Profit	$211,421
Expenses	<$189,501>
Net Profit	$ 21,920
Interest	$ 4,533
Taxes	---
EBIT	26,453
Depreciation	4,809
Amortization	1,668
EBITDA	$ 32,930
Owner's Salary	18,000
Non-Recurring Expenses	502
Building Rent	< 10,238>
Net Adjustments to EBITDA	$ 8,264
CASH FLOW	$ 41,194

Cash Flow is reduced to $41,194. Next, estimate and deduct management compensation to determine the business free cash flow – its earning power. When the business cash flow is adjusted for management compensation of $31,500, free cash flow becomes $9,694. Now apply this and other variables to a valuation formula to estimate a new business value.

210

Capitalization Method

Recall the cap rate for a business is 11.5%. Thus:

CAPITALIZATION METHOD

$$\frac{\$9,694\ (I)}{11.5\%\ (R)} = \$84,296 \text{ (Value without Real Estate)}$$

Excess Earnings Method

Using this method requires creation of another important valuation variable - a Risk/Price Multiple. An effective approach to developing this value involves rating key areas of business operation. These are: finance, control, marketing, sales, production, and service. Sub-elements of each may be rated on a scale of 1-5 where the higher number indicates less risk and better value. The average of all sub-elements and all six key areas have produced a business RPM that is 2.57. This stays unchanged, since it is assumed a buyer would have control over the property by lease.

EXCESS EARNINGS METHOD		
Variables		
Free Cash Flow		$93,94
Safe Rate of Return		6%
Tangible Assets		$60,000
Management Compensation		$31,500
RPM		2.57
Business Free Cash Flow		$ 9,694
Tangible Assets	60,000	
Safe Rate of Return	6.00%	
Return on Tangible Assets		< 3,600>
Business Excess Earnings		$ 6,094
Risk/Price Multiple		2.57
Value of Excess Earnings		$ 15,662
Value of Tangible Assets		60,000
ESTIMATED BUSINESS VALUE		$ 75,662

Leveraged Cash Flow Method

This method of valuing a small business has two variations. Both are designed to estimate business value by determining a reasonable amount of financing a business can pay using free cash flow. Equity is added to the calculated resulting debt to determine the business value.

One variation of the Leveraged Cash Flow method involves use of commercial financing. This option is not considered for this exercise because the debt coverage ratio (DCR) and loan-to-value (LTV) ratios will reduce financing significantly. For example, an LTV of 50% on inventory and furnishings makes only $30,000 of financing available. Financial leverage is lost unless a seller offers secondary financing. Under these conditions, using a loan term and

212

interest rate identical to those offered by a bank, the business estimated value would be the same as if the seller financed the purchase price him or herself – the second variation of the leveraged cash flow method. That option is illustrated below. Note, however, although the business values using seller or bank financing are the same, the latter could produce roughly $60,500 of cash at closing if exercised (double the amount produced by the seller-financed option).

LEVERAGED CASH FLOW METHOD (Seller Financing)	
VARIABLES:	
Free Cash Flow	$ 9,694
RPM	2.57
Tangible Assets	$ 60,000
Management Compensation	$ 31,500
Step 1: Calculate Monthly Payments For Debt	
Free Cash Flow	$ 9,694
(÷) Payments per period	(÷) 12
Monthly Payments	$ 807.83
Step 2: Determine Amount of Financing	
Interest Rate	9.75%
Loan Term	7
Monthly Payment	$ 807.83
Balance on Due Date	0
Serviceable Debt	$49,041.94
Step 3: Determine Business Value	
Affordable Loan Balance	$49,041.94
(+) Equity (Mgt. Comp. X 1.00)	$ 31,500.00
BUSINESS VALUE	$80,541.94

Note: It is possible to calculate equity using a business RPM, thus bringing a consistent approach to this step in the valuation formula. The amount of equity, expressed as a percentage of management compensation, is derived from the following table.

CALCULATING EQUITY From Risk/Price Multiples	
Business RPM	Equity
0.00 to 1.00	0% to 50%
1.01 to 2.00	51% to 75%
2.01 to 3.00	76% to 100%
3.01 to 4.00	101% to 125%
4.01 to 5.00	126% to 150%

Market Value

Recalculating values without real estate will produce the following value range.

CALCULATED VALUES Without Real Estate	
Capitalization Method	$ 84,296
Excess Earnings Method	$ 75,662
Leveraged Cash Flow (Seller Financed)	$ 80,542

Using measures of central tendency the business market value is estimated to be $79,979.

RANGE ANALYSIS To Determine Market Value	
Mean Value	$ 80,167
Range	$ 8,634
Median of Range	$ 4,317
Low Value in the Range	$ 75,662
Market Value of Business (Median)	$ 79,979

Reality Check

This market value is $2,927 _greater_ than the value indicated by simply subtracting the real estate market price from the value for both business and property. Moreover this latter business value is equally likely to pass the valuation tests of educated qualified buyers. The exercise reveals the business market value without real estate is $79,979 – much less than the $182,052 package price. Many more buyers can afford to buy the business by itself. Notice also, business good will is increased. With $60,000 of tangibles included, good will is increased by 17.2% from $17,052 in the combined sales price to $19,979 when the business is sold separately.

The business price without real estate still offers the seller plenty of equity, income from reasonable financing (if seller financing is elected) and lease payments on the building. In the future, this stream of monthly payments can be used to justify the sale of that asset to another investor. More likely, however, the buyers of the business will seek to acquire it themselves.

215

Develop Alternative Sales Options

Separating a business from its real estate can make both properties a more attractive investment offering. Marketing resources expended to sell a business are more effective when there is a target buyer in mind. Generally, there are strategic and financial buyers. This strategy can be used to attract either. More importantly, with the concept of selling the business and real estate separately, and the potential target buyers for each defined, a wider variety of sales options become possible.

Sell the Business/Hold the Real Estate

Burnout often associated with the desire to sell a business should not be allowed to affect the investment in its location. The benefits of commercial real estate ownership include cash flow, tax incentives, amortization and appreciation. Performance leases, remaining depreciation, amortization and a location in the path of progress may make holding the property a wise move. Simply selling the business may not erase these benefits. Sellers may want to hold the real estate and decide whether or not to sell it at a later date.

Holding the real estate after selling the business can also be an efficient tax strategy. Selling the business this year and the property in a later tax year may help hold down capital gains income. If this reduces marginal tax rates an attractive tax savings may occur.

Build In a Buyer for Both Properties

For all the reasons a seller acquired the business first and the real estate later, a new owner may do the same. The opportunity to set the stage for this event is presented when a business is sold and the property is leased to the buyer. By including a percentage lease rent rate, the cost of occupancy will increase if the business grows. At some

216

point the business operator may realize that owning the property would be less costly. Acquiring it becomes an obvious strategy to pursue. An option to buy at a predetermined price formula, or a first right of refusal in the lease, helps make this possible. In the mind of the business buyers, they have already laid a future claim to the property.

Sell the Business/Exchange the Real Estate for Another Investment

It may be possible to sell the business, creating cash, and exchange the real estate for like-kind investment property. This would be done when the business seller wants to remain active in the investment market but has exhausted the benefits of the current holding. Internal Revenue Code Section 1031 (IRC 1031) specifically deals with the exchange of investment property. The tax code language is straightforward: "No gain or loss shall be recognized on the exchange of property held productive use in a trade or business or for investment if such property is exchanged solely for property of like-kind which is to be held for productive use in a trade or business or for investment."

Knowledgeable real estate investors have used IRC Code Section 1031 exchanges for many years to avoid capital gains tax on the sale of real property. The advantage of tax deferment available to owners of real estate is also available on the sale of personal property. While exchanges of real property are more common sellers of business assets can exchange into a more desirable or profitable replacement property without losing their equity to capital gains taxes. Because a lifestyle change, or retirement, is often a motive to sell their business this tactic works best with the real estate.

A Purchase and Sale Agreement should contain language establishing the exchanger's intent and notifying the buyer of the exchange. Examples when selling are, "It is the intent of the Seller to perform an IRC Section 1031 tax-deferred exchange by trading the property herein with a qualified intermediary. Buyer agrees to execute an Assignment Agreement at the request of the Seller at no additional cost or liability to the Buyer." With this language in place the seller of the investment property may proceed to execute the remaining requirements of a tax-deferred exchange.

To illustrate the potential value of a tax-deferred exchange of the real property, assume its fair market value is $105,000 and the adjusted basis is $58,167. Long-term capital gains rates vary for most investors based on the applicable federal depreciation, appreciation and state tax rates. A range of from 20% to 25% is common, thus, a blended rate of 22.5% is used for the following illustration.

Fair Market Value of Real Estate	$ 105,000
Adjusted Basis	< 58,167>
Taxable Capital Gain	$ 46,833
Applicable Tax Rate	22.5%
Capital Gains Tax	$ 10,537
Taxes Deferred as Equity	$ 10,537

Combining the benefits of an asset separation strategy ($2,927) with a tax-deferred exchange ($10,537) increases equity after a sale/exchange by $13,464. Tax Deferred Exchanges are detailed in Chapter 19.

Sell the Property/Hold the Business

It is amazing that so many entrepreneurs succeed at the improbable task of building a business without ever knowing what it is worth. The valuation of a business separately from real estate often uncovers hidden potential. With this new information, some sellers become re-energized enough to continue developing unrealized growth potential. This may require cash. Holding the business while selling the real estate and leasing it back is a common tactic. With a track record of favorable business performance, investors are likely to have greater confidence in the financial capability of a tenant. A premium for the real estate is often paid. Sales proceeds can be invested to stimulate continuing business growth.

Separation of the real estate from the business is a powerful strategy that accomplishes many objectives. It makes a property more marketable, saves valuable time, and has the potential to increase business value. It is a special situation all business sellers who own a business and its location should strongly consider.

Rochelle Stone, President and CEO of Starker Services, Inc, contributed to this article. Starker Services is America's premiere Tax-Deferred Exchange third party intermediary with representation in 23 states. They may be contacted at their headquarters in Los Gatos, California by calling 800-332-1031.

Exchange To Avoid
The Tax Axe

"Silencing the silent partner"

As previously discussed, a unique approach is taken when the same person owns both the business and the real estate. The owner has more sales options, which can be appealing to potential buyers. Sometimes, especially in rural areas and in cases of many years of current ownership, the business and real estate are offered as a unit. The capital gain created can be large, so developing a sales strategy to minimize the effects of taxation is an important consideration.

Rather than sell the business or the real estate, it may also be possible to arrange a trade or exchange of properties with another entrepreneur or investor. Exchanges can be made between the business, the business real estate or both; the process is very tax efficient. Internal Revenue Code Section 1031 (IRC 1031) specifically deals

Note: Information in this chapter includes copyrighted material reprinted with permission from STARKER SERVICES, INC., America's premiere Tax Deferred Exchange third-party intermediary headquartered in Los Gatos, California (800- 332-1031). Starker has representation in 23 states to provide nationwide assistance to entrepreneurs and investors seeking to execute tax-deferred exchanges. As with all other material provided in this text, the material is for informational purposes only and not to be considered legal, accounting or tax advice. The reader is strongly advised to speak with a tax consultant before attempting to employ any of the information or concepts stated herein.

with the exchange of investment and business property. The tax code language is straightforward: "No gain or loss shall be recognized on the exchange of property held for productive use in a trade or business or for investment if such property is exchanged solely for property of like-kind which is to be held for productive use in a trade of business or for investment." No gain or loss shall be recognized. With no recognized gain the taxes are deferred until the property exchanged is sold. This is called a tax-deferred exchange. It creates added equity for the entrepreneur – a major financial benefit.

Business Exchanges

Knowledgeable real estate investors have used IRC Code Sec.1031 exchanges for many years to avoid capital gains tax on the sale of real property. On the other hand, many business proprietors and owners of capital assets have held business property for years because a sale translated into paying many thousands of dollars in capital gains tax. The advantage of tax deferment available to owners of real estate is also available on the sale of personal property under IRC Code Sec. 1031. Sellers of business assets can exchange into a more desirable or profitable replacement property without losing their equity to capital gains tax.

Tax Rates

Tremendous savings potential exists in exchanging a depreciated property with high residual value, as opposed to selling and paying the taxes. Since business assets are depreciated on a shorter schedule than real estate, depreciation recapture on the sale of personal property is taxed as ordinary income, which could be almost 39%. In addition, state taxes may be charged.

Restrictions

While the definition of like-kind property for real estate is very broad, the definition for personal property can be very restrictive. Treasury guidelines distinguish between depreciable tangible personal property and other personal property (such as intangible and nondepreciable property). When transferring depreciable business assets, the replacement property must fall into 1) the same "general asset" class or 2) the same "product" class. For example, a truck cannot be exchanged for computer equipment; a plane cannot be exchanged for construction equipment.

Asset Classes

The following is a list of 13 general asset classes:

✓ Furniture, fixtures and equipment

✓ Information systems (computers and peripherals)

✓ Data-handling equipment except computers

✓ Airplanes (noncommercial fixed wing) and helicopters

✓ Automobiles and taxis

✓ Buses

✓ Light general-purpose trucks

✓ Heavy general-purpose trucks

✓ Railroad cars and locomotives (except those owned by railroad transportation companies)

✓ Over-the-road tractor trailers

✓ Trailers and trailer-mounted equipment

✓ Water transportation equipment

✓ Industrial steam and electric generation and distribution systems

If the property being sold does not fall into the same "general asset" class as the replacement property, then it should fall into the same "product " class, published the North American Industry Classification System (NAICS) that replaces the U.S. Standard Industrial Classification (SIC) system.

Internet Reference

www.ntis.gov/naics

NAICS is the first-ever North American industry classification system. The system was developed by the U.S., Canada and Mexico to provide comparable statistics across the three countries. Government and business analysts will be able to directly compare industrial production statistics collected and published in the three North American Free Trade Agreement countries. NAICS also provides increased comparability with the International Standard Industrial Classification System (ISIC, Revision 3), developed and maintained by the United Nations.

Intangibles

Intangibles can be considered like-kind to other intangible property. The sale of a business such as a restaurant, hotel or dental practice normally involves intangible personal property, which is generally amortized, straight-line, for 15 years. Examples of intangibles include goodwill, covenants not to compete, franchise licenses, trade names, copyrights, client lists and going-concern values.

Tax counsel should be consulted to distinguish the intangibles that can be exchanged from those that cannot.

This is an area of considerable controversy, with conflicting case law. Generally, goodwill, covenants not to compete, going-concern value and customer lists are not considered property eligible for tax deferral. Franchises, trademarks, trade names and copyrights, among others, appear to be acceptable exchange property.

Allocation

Exchangers are usually motivated to allocate less value to assets that are non-qualifying – such as goodwill and inventory – to minimize taxable gain. Any allocation must be the same for the seller and the buyer of the property. Consequently, a buyer may not be a willing participant in arbitrary allocation. The IRC has the authority to review unreasonable allocations.

The sale of a business is actually treated as the sale of many assets. The tax code treats a business sale as the sale of each asset falling within a defined group (both tangible and intangible) to determine if there is a gain. All assets of the business must be itemized and placed into the appropriate asset or exchange group. Each exchange group will have either a surplus, if the replacement value is higher, or a deficiency, if the replacement value is less. There are two ways in which taxable "boot" is typically created: a deficiency (going down in value within a specific exchange group) and a residual group (where any non-matching asset is placed once the total value of each asset group is determined). Property (including money) within this group also results in taxable boot.

Additional property not eligible for exchange treatment is inventory. The inventory of a business is held for resale and does not fall within the like-kind definition of IRC 1031 property.

Here is an example of a potential business sale/exchange offered by Starker Services, Inc.:

and does not fall within the like-kind definition of IRC 1031 property.

Here is an example of a potential business sale/exchange offered by Starker Services, Inc.:

Sample Business Tax Deferred Exchange

A construction company sells for $734,000. The company's accountant determines the allocations for the main assets of the company as follows:

MAIN ASSETS
√   Three trucks valued at $33,000 each with an adjusted basis each of $15,000
√   One construction crane valued at $170,000 with an adjusted basis of $110,000
√   Two scrapers valued at $70,000 each with an adjusted basis each of $40,000
√   A cement truck valued at $75,000 with an adjusted basis of $50,000
√   A five-year covenant not to compete valued at $25,000 with an adjusted basis of $20,000
√   An airplane (used in normal business) valued at $200,000 with an adjusted basis of $125,000

If the construction company is sold with no exchange, and the fair market value of the equipment is greater than the depreciated basis of the equipment, ownership is facing capital gains taxes. The accountant calculates the gain for each asset class to determine the tax liability. Taxable gain is the variance between value and adjusted basis.

226

TAXABLE GAINS				
	VALUE	ADJUSTED BASIS	TAXABLE GAIN	TAXABLE BOOT
(3) General Purpose Trucks	$ 99,000	$ 45,000	$ 54,000	
(1) Crane	170,000	110,000	60,000	
(2) Scrapers	140,000	80,000	60,000	
(1) Cement Truck	75,000	50,000	25,000	
Goodwill	30,000	15,000		$ 15,000
Covenant not to Compete	25,000	20,000		5,000
Airplane	200,000	125,000	75,000	
TOTAL TAXABLE GAINS			$274,000	$ 20,000

An alternative to an outright sale would be to purchase another construction company in a different location. As a part of the purchase price, the sellers would receive same-asset-class replacements of equal or greater value, except for the airplane. The sellers must report gain on the sale of intangible assets (excluded property) and the airplane (residual group property). The remaining taxable gain is $199,000. Personal property assets are usually taxed at ordinary income tax rates. Assuming an applicable 31.5% rate, the taxes deferred are estimated at *$62,685*. Ownership may invest this as equity into another like-kind property instead of paying it as capital gains taxes. Employing the concept of the tax-deferred exchange can increase business equity and, ultimately, profitability.

Treasury Regulations

If exchanging an entire business, a single asset, or the business real estate, general rules will apply. Treasury regulations passed in 1991 allow for the exchange of property to give entrepreneurs and real estate investors choosing to use IRC 1031 access to benefits described. In general the rules are as follows:

✓ Exchangers must identify in writing the property they wish to exchange into (buy) within 45 days from the sale of their existing property. Identification is made to the intermediary.

✓ Exchangers may identify up to three properties they would be interested in purchasing with no limit on value, and they may purchase one, two or all three properties. If they want to identify more than three properties, the aggregate gross value of the identified properties cannot be more than 200% of the property being exchanged, unless the 95% rule applies.

✓ The 95% rule was introduced in Treasury Regulations on April 25, 1991. This regulation states if more than three properties are identified and the aggregate fair market value exceeds 200% of the property being exchanged, the exchanger must purchase 95% of the property identified.

✓ Exchangers have 180 days from the time they exchange out of their existing property (sale completed) to the purchase of a new property. Notice this means someone can sell his or her property to one party and allow the sales proceeds to remain in the possession of a qualified third party intermediary while searching for another property. The buyer is not required to have a property that will be exchanged.

✓ A qualified intermediary as described in the regulations will be able to handle the other details to ensure the exchange meets IRC-approved format. Individuals having a personal or professional relationship with the exchanger cannot act as a qualified intermediary. With few exceptions, the following are not permitted to act as intermediaries:

- A family member;

- A controlled corporation, partnership or trust related to the exchanger;

228

- Anyone considered an agent of the entrepreneur (such as his or her accountant, attorney or real estate agent).

The toughest part of the IRC 1031 exchange as it applies to personal property is the regulation of "like-kind." As generous as the definition is for real (estate) property, it is very narrow when it comes to personal property. This was demonstrated in the construction company example. Use of IRC 1031 to exchange the Bell-Quest, Ltd. (without real estate) example would not provide significant benefits to the entrepreneur. This is because goodwill and inventory are likely to be considered the bulk of fair market value exchanged.

Real Estate Exchanges

For real property to be "like-kind" it need only be "property used to produce income, used in a trade or business or held for investment purposes." This broad definition allows entrepreneurs to sell a business separately and exchange the real estate for an apartment building, a rental house, a shopping center or commercial building, an office or industrial building, or for commercial land.

Business owners discovering the high cost of capital gains taxes may want to seriously consider separating business from real estate. Applying the installment sale method to the business and a tax-deferred exchange to the real estate may produce an overall sales strategy that is very tax efficient. Those who own both real estate and business have a unique opportunity to explore this approach.

Taking the simplest approach, the fair market value of Bell-Quest, Ltd.'s building is $105,000; the adjusted basis is $58,167. Long-term capital gains tax rates are 20%. The deferral of capital gains taxes created by a tax-deferred exchange is calculated as follows. The adjusted basis is subtracted from the building's fair market value to determine the taxable capital gain. This is multiplied by the applicable long-term capital gains tax rate. The result is the amount of taxes that might have been due if not deferred by use of an IRC Code Sec. 1031 Tax-Deferred Exchange.

DEFERRED TAXES	
Fair Market Value of Real Estate	$105,000
Adjusted basis	< 58,167>
Taxable capital gain	46,833
Applicable tax rate	20%
Capital gain taxes	$ 9,367
Taxes deferred	$ 9,367

In the original business value placed on the business with real estate, the equity received as a down payment was approximately $30,500. The Tax Deferred Exchange has the potential to increase equity by 31%. This is a sales tactic all sellers with business real estate and qualifying tangible personal property should investigate as part of their preparation to sell a business.

Appendix A

Business Valuation Forms

Shortcut to Estimate Business Cash Flow
Earnings Reconstruction Formula
Calculating Business RPM Pricing Multiple

Formulas to Challenge and Reduce Value
- ✓ Capitalization Method
- ✓ Excess Earnings Method
- ✓ Leveraged Cash Flow Method (Seller Financing)
- ✓ Leveraged Cash Flow Method (Bank Financing)

Due Diligence Checklists
- ✓ Finance
- ✓ Control
- ✓ Marketing
- ✓ Sales
- ✓ Production
- ✓ Service

SHORTCUT TO ESTIMATE CASH FLOW

This technique is used to develop a rough estimate of a business cash flow with limited information. It works well because sellers do not feel answers to questions asked will be too revealing. Knowing how to calculate cost of goods from revenue and a percent markup is the key. This technique is fully described in Chapter Three. To develop the estimate the entrepreneur asks three questions and performs four simple steps listed below. Answers may be received by asking a seller during an initial meeting.

✓ "How much is the average revenue per month?"

✓ "What is the average markup on merchandise sold?"

✓ "On average, what are the cash expenses of the business, excluding owner's salary, each month?"

STEP 1: Calculate Cost of Goods.

Revenue ÷ 1.00 + Percent of Markup = Cost of Goods

$50,000 ÷ 1.00 + .30 (130%) = $38,451.54

STEP 2: Calculate business Gross Profit

Revenue − Cost of Goods = Gross Profit

$50,000 - $38,451.54 = $11,548.46

232

STEP 3: Calculate Estimate of Business Cash Flow

Gross Profit – Expenses = Cash Flow

$11,548.46 - $6,000 = $5,548.46

STEP 4: Estimate Annual Cash Flow

Monthly Cash Flow x Months Per Year = Annual Cash Flow

$5,548.46 x 12 = $66,581.52

SUBJECT PROPERTY: _____ DATE:_____

EARNINGS RECONSTRUCTION
Period: _____ to _____

Revenue		$_____
Cost of Goods	<$_____>	
Gross Profit		$_____
Expenses	<$_____>	
Net Profit		$_____
Interest	$_____	
Taxes	$_____	
EBIT (Earnings Before Interest & Taxes)		$_____
Depreciation	$_____	
Amortization	$_____	
EBITDA (EBIT, plus Depreciation & Amortization)		$_____
Positive Adjustments		
Education	$_____	
Employee Benefits	$_____	
Entertainment	$_____	
Home Office	$_____	
Mortgage Interest	$_____	
Non-Recurring Expenses	$_____	
Payroll (Owners Plus/Minus Other)	$_____	
Transportation	$_____	
Travel	$_____	
_____	$_____	
_____	$_____	
Negative Adjustments		
_____	<$_____>	
_____	<$_____>	
_____	<$_____>	
Net Adjustments		$_____
BUSINESS CASH FLOW		$_____

SUBJECT PROPERTY: _____ DATE:_____

BUSINESS RPM (Pricing Multiple) CALCULATOR
Period: _____ to _____

FINANCE   _____
Trailing Revenue   _____
Revenue Momentum   _____
Capital Structure   _____
Leverage Opportunities   _____
Earnings & Cash Flow   _____

CONTROL   _____
Employee Turnover Rate
& Cost (ETOR/ETOC)   _____
Employee Compensation   _____
Contingency Planning   _____
Network Penetration   _____
Potential Litigation   _____

MARKETING   _____
Well-Defined Marketing Plan   _____
Branded Power   _____
Market Differentiation   _____
Market Segmentation   _____
E-Commerce Activity   _____

SALES   _____
Type of Service or Product   _____
Sales Process Fit   _____
Sales Incentives Available   _____
Sales Training Programs   _____
Wired Distribution   _____

PRODUCTION   _____
Emphasis on Quality   _____
Innovation   _____
Capacity Vs Demand   _____
Obsolescence   _____
Inventory Management   _____

SERVICE   _____
Integrated Vision   _____
Employee Recognition   _____
Team Spirit   _____
Flexibility   _____
Open Communication   _____

INTELLECTUAL CAPITAL (Optional)   _____
Customer Satisfaction   _____
Employee Motivation   _____
Potential Synergies   _____
Key People   _____
Institutional Intelligence   _____

BUSINESS RPM (Pricing Multiple)   _____

SUBJECT PROPERTY: _____ DATE:_____

CAPITALIZATION METHOD OF VALUE
Period: _____ to _____

I (income) $ _____

R (rate)   _____%

V (value) $ _____

$$\frac{I}{R \times V}$$

Note#1
- ✓ Income divided by Rate equals Value
- ✓ Income divided by Value equals Rate
- ✓ Rate times Value equals Income

Note #2 - To calculate business values when one is not given, select a capitalization rate. Use Free Cash Flow as Income.

To challenge a given business value, solve for rate. Compare this to investor expectations. Or, solve for income and compare it to the actual free cash flow available.

When differences between expected and actual rate/income exist, substitute the market rate expected for the rate offered and solve for the indicated business value.

SUBJECT PROPERTY: _____ DATE:_____

EXCESS EARNINGS METHOD OF VALUE
Period: _____ to _____

Variables

Free Cash Flow	$_____	Safe Rate	_____%
Tangible Assets	$_____	RPM	_____

Business Free Cash Flow	$_____
Tangible Assets	$_____
(x) Safe Rate of Return	_____%
Return on Tangible Assets	$_____ <$_____>

Business Excess Earnings	$_____
(x) RPM (Pricing Multiple)	_____
Value of Excess Earnings	$_____
(+) Value of Tangible Assets	$_____

ESTIMATED BUSINESS VALUE	$_____

Excess Earnings Challenge

Business Value	$_____
(-) <u>Market Value of Tangible Assets</u>	<$_____>
Value of Excess Earnings	$_____

Value of Excess Earnings	$_____
(÷) Amount of Excess Earnings	$_____
RPM (Pricing Multiple)	_____

Note#1 - Substitute Actual RPM for indicated and recalculate value of excess earnings and business value.

SUBJECT PROPERTY: _____ DATE:_____

LEVERAGED CASH FLOW^{SF} METHOD OF VALUE
Period: _____ to _____

Variables:

Free Cash Flow $_____	RPM _____
Tangible Assets $_____	Mgt. Comp. $_____

STEP 1: Calculate Monthly Payments For Debt
Free Cash Flow $_____
(÷) <u>Payments per period</u> (Annual = 12)   _____
Monthly Payment Amount $_____

STEP 2: Determine Amount of Financing
Interest Rate   _____%
Loan Term   _____
Monthly Payment $_____
Balance on Due Date $_____
Serviceable Debt $_____

STEP 3: Determine Business Value
Serviceable Debt (Financing) $_____
(+)<u>Equity ("X" times Management Comp.)</u> $_____
BUSINESS VALUE $_____

Note #1- Substitute variables and terms of finance and recalculate for value. Compare against the asking price to challenge its accuracy.

Note #2 - The superscript "SF" in the title indicates this formula is generally used with seller financing where financing is secured from only one source.

SUBJECT PROPERTY: _____ DATE:_____

LEVERAGED CASH FLOW^{BF} METHOD OF VALUE
Period: _____ to _____

VARIABLES:

Free Cash Flow	$_____	RPM	_____
Tangible Assets	$_____	Mgt. Comp. $_____	
DCR	_____	LTV	_____%

STEP 1: Calculate Monthly Payments For Debt

Free Cash Flow	$_____
(÷) Payments per period (Annual = 12)	_____
Monthly Payment Amount	$_____

STEP 2: Determine Amount of Financing

	1st Mortgage	2nd Mortgage
Interest Rate	_____%	_____%
Loan Term (years)	_____	_____
Monthly Payment	$_____	$_____
Balance on Due Date	$_____	$_____
Serviceable Debt	$_____	$_____

STEP 3: Determine Business Value

Combined Serviceable Debt (Financing)	$_____
(+)Equity ("X" times Management Comp.)	$_____
BUSINESS VALUE	$_____

Note #1- Substitute variables and terms of finance and recalculate for value. Compare against the asking price to challenge its accuracy.

Note #2- The superscript "BF" in the title indicates this formula is generally used with bank financing. This often results in more than one loan – the seller often takes a second.

SUBJECT PROPERTY: _____ DATE:_____

DUE DILIGENCE CHECKLISTS
(An asterisk "*" denotes key information needed)
Period: _____ to _____

FINANCE CHECKLIST
1. Contact Persons. (name, address, phone, fax and e-mail of each)
___Business principal*
___General manager
___In-house bookkeeper
___Certified public accountant
___Banking representative

2. Mortgages and Notes Payable
___Principal Balances*
___Term of loan/interest rate/payment amount
___Payoff date and penalties associated
___Collateral pledges
___Identity of persons signing and guaranteeing payment

3. Leases for Location and Equipment
___Description of location or materials covered by the lease
___Amount of lease payments due*
___Payment schedules
___Term of the lease and options to renew
___Responsibilities (who pays for what)

4. Accounts Receivable/Payable
___Amount of each*
___Separate each into 30, 60, 90 and Over 90 days due
___Historical record of changes in both
___Ratio of accounts receivable to accounts payable over time*
___Collection procedures

___Cash or accrual method of accounting used
___Estimate of revenue from work under contract but not performed*
___Estimate of work to be performed eventually but not under contract

5. Financial Statements
___Balance sheets for three to five years*
___P&L Statements for three to five years*
___Tax returns for three to five years

6. Credit
___Credit history of the business
___Amount of credit available from suppliers and vendors
___Terms of credit available from suppliers and other vendors

CONTROL CHECKLIST

1. Ownership Structure
___Form of ownership*
___Articles of incorporation; partnership and/or shareholder agreement
___Name of principals with more than 25 percent ownership*
___Name of minority shareholders
___List of shareholders not employed by the business
___Organization chart
___Fictitious name registrations

2. Strategic Alliances
___Vendor relationships
___Franchise agreements*
___Marketing and advertising agencies
___Accounting firms
___Law firms
___Commitments of time and money vs. services rendered from above
___Company attorney

___Insurance agent

3. Employee Relationships
___Employment contracts
___Independent contractors and agreements
___Employee manual
___Job descriptions
___Estimate of employee turnover rate and cost (ETOR and ETOC)*
___Procedure to locate, assess and hire employees
___Enforceable covenants not to compete
___Employee training programs

4. Location
___Property survey
___Zoning classification and restrictions
___Easements on the property
___Real estate taxes
___Property appraisal*
___Buildings and improvements*
___Floor plan of buildings and location of improvements

5. Administrative
___Licenses
___Insurance plans and policies
___Pending litigation*
___Contingent liabilities*
___Internet or Intranet-enabled administration procedures and
   protocols

MARKETING CHECKLIST
1. Business Mission Statement

2. Marketing Position

3. Marketing & Communication Strategy

___Advertising and marketing themes and appeals*
___Venues for spreading the marketing message
___Advertising contracts
___Agreements with advertising or marketing firms or agents
___Samples of marketing and advertising materials
___Marketing research to support position and strategy*

4. E-commerce applications
___Web site address*
___# of hits per day
___Conversion rate of hits to sales*
___Links to other web site providers
___Describe business-to-business activity

5. Competitive marketing analysis
___Description of nearest competitor
___Number or competitors in trade area
___Market share*
___Marketing opportunities to expand current sales results

6. Growth Wall Analysis*
___Negative Trend of Sales and Profits
___Obsolescence of Product or Service Line
___Unproductive Advertising & Marketing
___Declining Employee Morale
___No Enhancements to Product or Services

"A growth wall is a common condition that prevents progress and results. It stops a business dead in its tracks. The most obvious symptom is the end of a strong favorable trend of trailing revenue. It occurs because the environment around a business has changed but the business has not. For example, selling 8-track tape players was big business in the 1960s. Companies still attempting to sell them today would likely fail. The market has changed. Thus, a growth wall presents considerable increase in business risk."

It is important to recognize growth walls in business valuation because a declining trend of business results often prompts an owner to consider selling their business. Value is falling. An entrepreneur, recognizing this phenomenon, is better armed to make adjustments that could return the business to an upward performance trend.

"Professor Richard Osborne, case Western Reserve University, describes the phase two (after the start-up has already passed) growth wall as common in the evolution of owner managed entrepreneurial companies. He notes several patterns inherent in companies that fail to penetrate a growth wall, including 1) sudden reversals in revenue after steady annual business increases; 2) diminished entrepreneurial energy; 3) generalized internal focus; 4) falling behind the industry trend change curve; 5) reactive product or service development, distribution, and marketing; and 6) absence of internal attitudes and competencies necessary to see and understand external threats."

"To break through a growth wall, company managers must reestablish the link between their product and their market – the latter has changed and the former has not. Business managers should study the environment in which the business operates to identify and recommend complimentary changes. The entrepreneur who can recognize a growth wall in a business, and has the ability to scale it, may enjoy highly lucrative business investment opportunities."

SALES CHECKLIST

1. Sales Results*
___Sales data*
___Annual trends
___Seasonal trends
___Time to create one sale
___Average sales price
___Average gross profit per sale
___Average net profit per sale
___Impact of sales cycles on cash flow*
___Record of cash flows by month*
___Record of deficit spending to sustain low sales months

2. Description of Product or Service
___Transactional products
___Consulting services
___Enterprise relationships
___Key benefit to customer*

3. Sales Channels
___How are sales leads generated*
___How are sales made*
___Sales persons
___Telemarketing
___Direct mail
___Internet
___Other

4. Sales Management
___Sales lines of authority
___Sales person or employee span of control*
    ___Number of accounts one can handle
    ___Amount of sales floor one can handle
___Sales compensation formula*
___Base compensation
___Commission income
___Territorial assignments
___Geographically based
___Product based
___Treatment of reimbursable expenses
___Description of sales training

PRODUCTION CHECKLIST
1. Production
___Capacity to produce under existing conditions
___Limitations on capacity

___Variance between existing capacity and demand*
___Cost to increase capacity

2. List of Property
___Equipment
___Furnishings
___Fixtures
___Description of each of above
___Age and condition of equipment
___Obsolescence noted*
___Deferred maintenance noted*

3. Inventory
___Amount on hand to meet existing demand*
___End of year (EOY) changes in quantity of inventory on hand
___Inventory turnover ratio*
___Annual cost of goods / inventory at cost
___Accounting systems to identify inventory on hand and needed
___Variance of inventory in peak versus low selling seasons
___Source of Inventory and timing of delivery

4. Schematic of Work Flow
___Receipt of inventory
___Storage of inventory
___Description of production process if any*

SERVICE CHECKLIST
1. Services
___Services performed*
___Pricing structure for services
___Turnaround time for service work
___Who performs services to clients

2. Policies

___Product or service guarantees
___Returns & refunds*
___Payment
___Tracking system
___Managing complaints
___Annual cost of returns

3. Distribution of Service
___Where service is performed
___Profitability of service
___How products are returned
___Who pays cost of shipping

4. Training*
___Staff training of new personnel
___Employee education and seminars
___Outsourced service department

5. Intellectual Capital
___Unique sources*
___Key people
___Patents & copyrights
___Production processes
___Competitive intelligence
___Customer relationships*
___Institutionalized or related to key people
___Transferability of intellectual capital
___Control over intellectual capital
   ___Vested rights
   ___Non-disclosure agreements with key personnel

Appendix B

GENERAL TERMS AND FEATURES OF ACQUISITIONS

This material is for general information purposes only. Laws governing small business acquisitions and dispositions change periodically. State laws affecting these issues vary widely. This material is not to be considered as legal, accounting or tax advice. Readers are strongly advised to speak with their respective legal, accounting or tax consultants before attempting to employ any of the information or concepts stated herein.

ACQUISITION AGREEMENT - When the buyer and seller reach an agreement to transfer a business, by the basic structure of this transaction (terms and conditions), a written acquisition agreement should be prepared. Generally buyers prepare the initial acquisition agreement since it is they who are advancing an offer.

Many acquisition agreements are prepared on a standard form. These can be effective, provided they meet all the needs of the parties involved. Many do not. Most, however, will share the same elements, which are listed here.

- ✓ Identity of assets or stock to be sold, the price and terms, and the mechanics or rules governing the transaction

- ✓ Other conditions of the agreement including, but not limited to, amount of earnest money or deposit delivered with the acquisition agreement, financing, provisions for a covenant not to compete, training to be provided by the seller, earn-out provisions, etc.

✓ Representations and warranties of the seller (e.g., when real estate is included, the seller may warrant title to the property is good and marketable)

✓ Representations and warranties of the buyer

✓ Covenants pending a closing

✓ Conditions precedent to a closing

✓ Provisions of the closing or termination of the agreement (e.g., setting the time and place of closing, form of funds to be brought to the closing, etc.); also, may include a penalty for failure to close when all other conditions of the agreement have been satisfied –often forfeiture of a percentage of the sales price, which may be taken from the deposit

✓ Indemnifications of the parties involved (buyer to seller; seller to buyer; both to lender, their professional representatives, etc.)

✓ Provision of payment for fees, expenses and other miscellaneous matters

ACQUISITION OF ASSETS VS. STOCK – Many small businesses are closely held. This means they have a small number of owners or are family owned. They may be incorporated, too. When acquiring a business that has been incorporated, most buyers prefer to acquire the assets from the corporation or partnership instead of the stock in the legal entity. This occurs because the company, not its stockholders, owns the business assets. The stockholders own stock in the company. Here are two important reasons.

When acquiring assets, buyers establish a new value for depreciable tangible and intangible assets being purchased. It may be larger than the property's basis under current

250

ownership. The new, greater value increases the amount of depreciation or amortization that may be taken by a buyer. This often compares favorably to the remaining tax benefit available to the corporation that owns the assets.

Also, there may be certain liabilities that accompany ownership of a corporation. These may be outstanding financial obligations or existing and potential liabilities created by lawsuits. These can pass to a buyer as the new owner of stock in the company.

To avoid unintended assumption of liabilities and establish a new basis for depreciation of assets, buyers often elect to buy business assets rather than outstanding stock.

ALLOCATION OF PRICE - The sale of a business involves the sale of tangible and intangible assets. The total of all property acquired is the purchase price. The purpose of the allocation is to establish a new basis for depreciation and amortization based on the fair market value of the property involved.

As a condition precedent to closing, a value must be placed on each asset acquired – both tangible and intangible. Both parties must agree to the allocation, which can have varying tax consequences for each. Allocation should be done by the parties' tax consultants or other qualified professional representatives. The Internal Revenue Service has the authority to review allocations it considers unreasonable.

APPRAISAL - As a condition precedent to a closing, a property appraisal is often requested to confirm value. A buyer, seller or lender providing financing to the buyer acquiring property may require this. Payment for the appraisal may be negotiated between the parties. In those cases where a business acquisition is contemplated, business valuation skill on the part of the buyer or lender will be most helpful. The supply of qualified business appraisers is small to nonexistent in rural areas.

APPROVALS - Prior to closing many approvals may be needed. These are conditions precedent to a closing. Typical approvals needed for most acquisitions are:

✓ Approval of licensing or franchising authorities

✓ Approval of lender for financing

✓ Approval of buyers' or their professional representatives' review of financials and all other aspects of the business operation and its operating agreements

✓ Approval of the buyer's financial qualifications where seller financing is involved

✓ Approval of stockholders when necessary.

As a general rule it is best to secure as many approvals as possible prior to the closing. This prevents last-minute changes that can often occur.

ASSUMPTION OF DEBT - Many times a business sold will have existing debt. Buyers may elect to assume the debt and, if so, should state the terms and conditions under which this may occur. Various questions should be considered. If debt assumption is to be renegotiated, when is this to be completed? Will the seller's guarantee be released or not? Is the buyer given permission to discuss the outstanding debt with the appropriate creditors?

In other instances, the buyer may want to acquire a business free and clear of debts, liens and encumbrances of any kind. Normally this is more to a buyer's liking and is especially preferred when a lender is providing acquisition financing. In such cases the agreement will discuss the nature, size and terms of outstanding business debts together with a condition that they will be paid in full at closing.

ASSUMPTION OF AGREEMENTS - A condition that provides for a buyer's assumption of agreements usually refers to a franchise agreement. It may also include special arrangements with business vendors or professionals representing the business whose involvement is to be continued. These would be noted in the acquisition agreement.

BILL OF SALE - A bill of sale is evidence a transfer of personal property has occurred. Because real estate is not included in the sale of many businesses, a bill of sales is a common form of conveyance. Where real estate is included, conveyance is by way of a deed.

BULK SALES LAW - Many states have a bulk sales law. This is commonly applied to transactions where an inventory for resale is included in the sale. The bulk sales provisions require that notification be given to a business's creditors prior to the sale of property or a business where credit has been extended. As a result, the creditor can make claims for payment prior to the closing.

The intended result of a bulk sales law is to draw a line between debts of the buyer and debts of the seller. Creditors are paid from the rightful debtor, and a business is conveyed without debts except those a buyer assumes and agrees to pay. In some states a Uniform Commercial Code provides for payment of creditors out of sales proceeds.

A problem with the bulk sales law occurs among buyers and sellers who do not want to notify creditors of a sale, thus losing confidentiality. This can be of particular concern to a seller when a closing remains in doubt. Buyers, on the other hand, do not want outstanding debts to surface as claims against them – the new owners of the business. Even when the buyer is not responsible for payment, creditors have been known to refuse delivery of additional merchandise until outstanding claims are paid by prior ownership or anyone else. As a compromise, some buyers and sellers circumvent the bulk sales provisions. The seller gives the buyer a list of outstanding business debts as of the closing and agrees to pay them from closing proceeds. Thereafter, he or she may be willing to escrow additional closing proceeds for a short time. These can be used to pay off other undisclosed debts if any are discovered. If none exist, escrowed funds are released to the seller. As an additional provision the seller may agree to indemnify and hold the buyer harmless for any liabilities incurred from creditor claims that originated prior to the closing.

COVENANTS PENDING A CLOSING - These are items that restrict or obligate buyer and seller to take, or to avoid taking certain actions prior to the closing. Restricting the release of information to parties to the transaction and their professional representatives might be one example. Other covenants might require the sellers to continue normal business operations, conducting no unusual activities such as a going-out-of-business sale; to keep the negotiations strictly confidential; to keep the business property well maintained and insured; and to make timely payment of all taxes and financial obligations prior to closing.

COVENANT NOT TO COMPETE - A covenant not to compete, or non-competition agreement, is generally given from a seller to a buyer. It is important when the seller possesses technical knowledge about the business being purchased that could be used by a competitor to attract the market share of the business. The result would be a reduction of revenue and performance created by the seller's actions after a closing.

Most covenants not to compete include four key provisions: a term, a geographic reference, the type of activity not permitted and a value. There may be other conditions as well, including remedies for violation of the covenant.

CONDITIONS PRECEDENT TO CLOSING -Actions a buyer or seller must, or must not do to accomplish an activity are conditions precedent to a closing. For example, buyers or their professional representatives must review and approve the business financials within 10 business days from the date the acquisition agreement is fully executed. Here is a partial list of the topics that might be included as a condition, that is to be performed or subject to review and approval. Note the list is by no means complete and could include many other conditions that might pertain to a unique buyer or business situation.

- ✓ Financing commitment
- ✓ Appraisal of property
- ✓ Financial statements review
- ✓ Business operations review
- ✓ Due diligence
- ✓ Training or training plan for buyer
- ✓ Credit, financial and qualifications of buyer
- ✓ Business, franchise and professional service agreements
- ✓ Review of customer and vendor lists
- ✓ Approvals from licensing and regulatory authorities
- ✓ Completed physical inventory and approval
- ✓ Review of all tangibles and intangibles
- ✓ Review of debt and liabilities assumed
- ✓ Bulk sales compliance

✓ Sales tax treatment of inventory purchased

✓ Certificate of good standing and all other documentation

EARNEST MONEY - When arranging transactions to sell and buy businesses and/or real estate, the ability to keep a transaction from falling apart is often related to the amount of earnest money placed on deposit by a buyer. When a substantial earnest money deposit is made, the buyer is more committed to perform. In such instances a seller also is more willing to take the buyer seriously than if a promissory note or a dollar bill is clipped to an offer.

Receipt and use of earnest money is a negotiable issue. It may be delivered in one or more installments. These can begin at the first execution date of the acquisition agreement and continue as conditions are completed in an orderly sequence. Earnest money may be refundable if certain conditions precedent to a closing remain unfulfilled by closing or a certain date stated earlier. Certain expenses, such as appraisal fees, may be deducted from the earnest money. In other instances, where conditions are fully executed, the earnest money is credited to the purchase price of the property.

EARN OUTS - An earn out is a form of payment buyers offer sellers where there is uncertainty about the future performance of a business. To implement an earn out strategy, the buyer will acquire the business and agree to pay additional premiums to the seller based on business results received. A simple form of earn out would be where the seller receives a small percentage of the increase in business revenue. If the results improve, the selling party is rewarded. If results decline, no additional payment is made.

Earn outs are a good way to test a seller's confidence in the future of a business. It is also helpful to keep a seller committed to work for the continued success of the enterprise. There is a direct financial incentive for this support.

EXPIRATION OF OFFERS - An expiration of offer occurs when the acquisition agreement includes a date by which a response from the seller is required. If none is received the offer is withdrawn. Buyers often place expiration dates in acquisition offers to encourage a timely response from sellers; if no response is received, they move on. Sometimes an expiration date is used to pressure a seller into quick acceptance. This tactic is unhelpful because it usually results in a seller's avoidance of the offer entirely, or their attachment of additional provisions that have a nullifying effect on the expiration date. The seller's response may also be accompanied by an equally short deadline for the buyer's acceptance of added provisions.

An expiration of offer that provides a seller with a reasonable amount of time to consider the proposition is an acceptable approach. Such an expiration should be included to prevent sellers from holding the offer indefinitely and attempting to find other offers that are better. Also, a reasonable expiration date, helps ensure the buyer's proposal is not accepted at a later time after the buyer has made an investment elsewhere.

FINANCING - Since most buyers of businesses want to use investment leverage in acquisitions, a condition providing them with a chance to secure a financing commitment is frequently included in an acquisition agreement.

Buyers often state very specific terms of financing requested. Sellers counter by adjusting them to reflect outside limits. For example, a seller might modify the buyer's statement of terms that seek financing at 9% annual interest rate to financing that does not exceed 10%. The difference is the buyer could use a commitment of financing at 8.5% as a device to avoid the contract *for any other reason.* The seller's approach would eliminate this loophole.

In general, when securing financing is a condition precedent to closing, the terms stated are amount, interest rate, loan term, method of payment, collateral and personal guarantees involved.

FUTURE BUSINESS ASSURANCES - Occasionally buyers ask sellers to state that they know of no events occurring or about to occur that could negatively affect business performance. This is not an unreasonable condition. Sellers respond, however, by stating that they are delivering the business "as is" and no warranties for future performance are made or implied. This is an important issue since the earnings reconstruction used in a business valuation process is designed to reveal the differences between taxable income and cash flow. As such it is not a tool to forecast the future. It is an indication of what has been and is, based entirely on trailing earnings. For this reason, sellers creating a value range based on next year's cash flow are well-advised to keep their cash flow forecasts to themselves. If desired, buyers should construct these with the help of their professional representatives.

More importantly, when a final or year-end financial statement is to be received between a letter of intent or acquisition agreement and closing, it is unwise to link approval of the business's financial condition to receipt of these documents. They could reveal a dramatic downturn in business. It is better to state the business results should reflect no change in business revenue or should include improvements that can be defined.

GOOD STANDING OF CORPORATION - States require corporations to pay what is commonly called a "franchise tax." This accompanies the ability of an entity to legally operate and conduct lawful business in the state in which it is licensed to operate.

A certificate of good standing is a statement from regulatory authorities to indicate a corporation is in compliance, taxes are paid and the entity is in "good standing." This certificate is often requested as a condition precedent to a closing. It ensures the corporation selling the assets has the authority to act.

INDEMNIFICATION - This is a condition whereby the parties to an agreement each agree to compensate the other for damages or losses that may occur. In an acquisition agreement the sellers would indemnify buyers against any losses that might occur as a result of debts not assumed by the buyer and unpaid by the seller.

How might this occur? Suppose a liquor store changes hands July 1 and the seller fails to pay an outstanding invoice for beer delivered. The new owner places an order for more stock to be received by July 3. The vendor refuses to deliver until the outstanding invoice is paid. The loss of sales can be substantial and, under certain conditions, the buyer might have a claim.

Pending litigation and undisclosed liabilities are common reasons a seller will indemnify a buyer. Brokers guiding a business transaction often state in the acquisition agreement that they have made no representations. They further state that execution of the agreement by the parties is their agreement to indemnify the broker against consequences of the transaction.

INSPECTIONS - Inspections may be a condition precedent to closing. Approvals often accompany the inspections as well as a date by which approval is to be received. Handled in this way the inspections are gradually removed and are no longer a roadblock to closing.

Inspections may include:

- ✓ business financials
- ✓ agreements such as including leases, franchises, employment contracts, professional service agreements, etc.
- ✓ business property, including real estate and improvements, furnishings, fixtures and equipment
- ✓ operating procedures.

INTANGIBLES - Property that contributes to business performance but cannot be touched or felt is intangible property. Covenants not to compete, goodwill, customer lists and a franchise are common forms of intangible assets. The acquisition agreement should state the intangibles acquired together with allocated values.

INVENTORY - Acquisition agreements for the purchase of a retail business will state, as a condition precedent to closing, the inventory must be counted just prior to closing. This provision will often name the service that will perform the inventory and govern the process. Both buyer and seller should be present at the inventory to approve of the process. Buyers many want to exclude certain types of inventory that appear damaged or dated.

When taking an inventory for most small businesses, the easiest method to use involves categorizing all merchandise by markup. For example, all merchandise in one category is marked up 30%, items in another category are marked up 40% and the rest is marked up 20%. Merchandise is counted at its retail value. Divide the total by 1.00 plus the percent of markup to identify actual cost of the merchandise. This is a simple and generally acceptable way to determine the value of inventory that will be included with the business at the closing, which should follow immediately.

When offered for sale, a business may be priced plus or including inventory at seller's cost. The difference can be meaningful when attempting to attract a buyer. One price is much lower but more uncertain; the other is higher but instills more confidence in the buyer. Using the latter, if the inventory at closing is less than the amount stated to be present in the acquisition agreement, the price is adjusted accordingly. If the amount of inventory is greater, the buyer may pay the added amount, issue a credit to the seller for merchandise in the future, or add the additional amount to seller financing if applicable.

LETTER OF INTENT - A letter of intent may be used as a precedent to an acquisition agreement. A buyer prepares a letter of intent, signs it and delivers it to the seller, who signs it, too. The letter of intent is executed prior to a formal acquisition agreement.

Letters of intent are helpful when there is a need to commit a basic agreement between buyer and seller to writing. This prevents future misunderstanding and helps avoid renegotiation. Also, a letter of intent conveys a moral commitment between the parties. To the extent that business people keep their word, a letter of intent is helpful to move a transaction along. Letters of intent generally have several common elements:

✓ A statement of whether the letter of intent is binding or not

✓ A statement of whether a formal acquisition agreement will be prepared, in which case the letter of intent is subject to that document's execution

    ✓ The form of the transaction: Is it an asset purchase, the purchase of a business with or without real estate, or a purchase of company stock?

    ✓ The price and terms

    ✓ Significant provisions, covenants and conditions precedent to execution of the acquisition agreement and/or a closing

For obvious reasons, letters of intent also are helpful when the time until an acquisition agreement is executed will be lengthy.

LIMITATION OF LIABILITY - One way entrepreneurs attempt to reduce exposure created by indemnifications is to establish an upper limit on their liability. This may be a reasonable request, provided the limit is established at an appropriate level. Some feel the liability should not exceed the value of property conveyed. Others feel the limit should be tied to historical limits, if they exist. In any case, when limitations on liability are introduced, the other party is given a reason for added concern.

    Also, when indemnity is given to prevent liability, parties attempt to secure joint and several liabilities. Normally this occurs when more than one individual is liable for an obligation. When used, all individuals are each liable for the entire obligation – not on their prorated share of the obligation. Thus, collection is easier because it is presumed certain members of a group who are jointly and severally liable will encourage full payment from the entire group.

MISREPRESENTATION - Buyers and sellers make statements about themselves and their businesses to each other. When it is discovered (usually by a due diligence or background check) that something has been omitted that should not have been, a misrepresentation may have occurred.

    The severity of misrepresentations is often determined by the intent or non-intent to omit information and whether it is material to the terms and conditions of the acquisition agreement or not. Where a misrepresentation is intentional and material, a buyer's typical recourse is to walk away from the transaction. If the transaction has already occurred, a buyer's recourse may include other legal remedies.

PHYSICAL CONDITION OF FIXED ASSETS - As a condition precedent to closing, a buyer may want assurances that all property purchased is in good working condition. Inspections are typical for real estate, and this may require wording to allow professional inspectors access to the property for the purpose of making specific inspections. These are often at the buyer's expense. A provision may be inserted into the agreement to resolve any dispute arising from assets found to be in poor condition.

REPRESENTATIONS - These are statements a seller usually makes to a buyer that indicate the condition of a business being acquired. They often refer to other statements – the financials of the business – and are subject to verification. Representations are normally tied to a date that has already passed. Changes after that date are the subject of additional disclosures.

RIGHT OF RECISION - Acquisition agreements for a small business may include a right of recision for the buyer. This means that within a specified period of time, usually determined by state statues, the buyer may elect to cancel the agreement. The term in which a right of recision may be exercised is usually short, 24 to 48 hours.

SALES TAXES - When the form of acquisition is an asset purchase, it may be necessary to state certain provisions to describe the purchase of inventory. This can be necessary because if improperly done, or omitted, a buyer purchasing inventory could be liable for payment of sales taxes on the entire amount purchased. This can be substantial. Because sales taxes are affected by state and local regulations, the buyer should investigate this carefully with local authorities.

TANGIBLES - Tangibles are the property being conveyed that has physical form and substance. This includes real property but, more specifically, refers to personal property such as business furnishings, fixtures, equipment, leasehold improvements and inventory. The acquisition agreement should allocate a reasonable value to each tangible asset conveyed in the transaction. This value normally becomes the basis used to calculate the amount of depreciation a buyer will receive in the future and the amount of gain a seller will receive from the sale.

TRAINING - Another provision of the acquisition agreement requires the seller to train the buyer in all aspects of business operations. When used, the amount and term of training should be specified. Also, sellers often receive compensation for their involvement. The acquisition agreement should indicate if this compensation is to be considered income or a part of the price paid for the business.

Appendix C

CHECKLIST OF TAX TERMS AND ISSUES

The United States Tax Code has many regulations that can change, sometimes frequently and with little notice. Building tax-efficient strategies offer the potential to minimize taxes and maximize profits. Entrepreneurs should develop a general awareness of tax strategies that work to their advantage and minimize the impact of taxes.

This material and information is not given as tax advice nor is it to be used as such. As with all information presented in this text, readers are advised to seek the guidance of a qualified professional representative or accountant.

The following is a checklist of some tax issues that may affect business acquisition, ownership and disposition. It includes a brief description of each item. Note, the tax code is several million pages. This material is for general information purposes only. It is intended to acquaint the reader with general concepts that may apply to business acquisition, management and dispositions.

Taxable Income

Tax Rates. Tax rates are the percent of qualifying income received in the fiscal or calendar year that will be paid in taxes. Tax rates vary according to the type of taxpayer. There are different rates for corporations, individual taxpayers, heads of households, and married taxpayers filing together or separately.

The current range of corporate tax rates is graduated from approximately 15 percent to 39 percent. For most individuals the range of tax rates is graduated from 15 percent to 39.6 percent. These rates change periodically. EBIT, or taxable earnings, produced by most small businesses is often passed to owners based on their prorated interest in the company. When business income is credited to owners it is taxed according to their individual applicable tax rates.

Taxable Income – Cash Basis - A business owner's method of accounting will determine the year in which income is considered taxable. The cash basis of accounting is used by most small businesses. With this method income is earned and taxable in same year it is received.

Taxable Income – Accrual Method - Income that becomes taxable when earned is an example of the accrual method of accounting. Income is earned when services or goods necessary to be exchanged for income have been delivered. Notice, with this method it is possible to earn taxable income without receiving the actual income until a later taxable year.

Capital Gains & Losses - A capital gain or loss occurs upon the sale of a capital asset. The Internal Revenue Code (IRC) states what is not a capital asset. This list generally includes business property such as inventory, depreciable business property, and business land not held for investment. The code attempts to distinguish between gains arising from capital appreciation versus normal business activity. The sale of inventory is considered business profit, not capital gain. The gain on antiques held for their investment potential may be a capital gain.

Capital gains are divided into two categories: short-term capital gain and long-term capital gain. The difference is created by the holding period. Generally, long-term capital gains receive more favorable tax treatment. The long-term capital gains tax rate for individual taxpayers is 20%; this changes from time to time. This compares very favorably to the higher rates that apply to ordinary income. A short-term capital gain is taxed the same as ordinary income.

Net Operating Losses - Net operating losses in a business occur when business expenses exceed the income for a taxable year. Net Operating Losses can be carried back to offset income received in previous years, creating a refund for the taxpayer. Net Operating Loses also can be carried forward and deducted from the income created in a future year. The result is a savings of taxes.

Passive Losses - Passive losses may occur with investments in which the entrepreneur does not play a material role or actively participate. Examples of passive income investments are apartment buildings and other types of commercial real estate investments. Prior to 1987 it was possible for high-income taxpayers to use a net operating loss from passive investments to offset income earned from their business or profession. The result was a savings of taxes. Passive investments providing net operating losses were called tax shelters.

The IRC states that the use of losses or tax credits created by passive investment activity cannot be used to reduce tax liability created by business income earned.

Taxable Treatment of Transactions

Sale or Exchange of Property - A sale of a property occurs when one receives cash, notes, or their equivalent in exchange for ownership of a property. Typically, an exchange occurs when one receives other property in the place of cash or its equivalent. A capital gain or loss may result from the sale or exchange of a property.

Holding Period for Property - The holding period of a property is the term of ownership from the date it is acquired until the date sold. The holding period determines if the gain upon sale is a short- or long-term gain. Thus, the holding period can have a significant impact on the taxable capital gain created.

Gain from the sale of property held for one year or less is a short-term capital gain. Gain from the sale of property held more than one year is a long-term capital gain. This means, if a property is sold on the one-year anniversary date of its acquisition, the capital gain will be short term. If the property is sold the day after the anniversary date of the date it was acquired, the capital gain is long term. The applicable tax rates can produce a major variance in taxes due.

Basis - The basis of a property is the cost paid for the property in cash or, in the event of an exchange, the market value of other property given. Basis can also include costs incurred to acquire and improve the property so it is suitable for use.

Realized Gain or Loss from the Sale of Property. A gain is realized when a sale of a property occurs and there is a difference between the net sales price and the basis. The total of cash and other property (at market value) received is used to determine the amount realized. Subtract basis from the amount realized to determine if a gain or loss occurs. Realized gains or losses do not occur with changes in the market value of a property. A sale or exchange triggers a realized gain.

Installment Sale Method - For many years sellers have enjoyed the benefits of seller financing to support their retirement objectives. With a modest down payment, monthly income can be received over several years. This is called the "installment sale" method of business disposition. It is a tax efficient strategy. Capital gains taxes are due only as payments have been collected.

An installment sale as defined by the IRC is, "a sale of property where at least one payment for the property is received after the year in which the sale occurs." Even a sale of property that is paid in a lump sum can be an installment sale if the lump-sum payment is received in a tax year that follows the year of sale. When sellers finance a property, they typically take from 20% to 40% of the purchase price as a down payment and "carry the balance" over a reasonable amount of time. This is an installment sale.

Favorable tax treatment is offered because a portion of the gross profit from the installment sale (profit in excess of basis) is included in the seller's income each year in which a payment for the property is received. As a result the taxpayer uses this installment method for reporting gross profit from qualifying installment sales. The amount of gross profit is not affected, however. This method only extends the time over which gross profit is received as taxable income. Therefore, the installment method permits payments of taxes due on the gross profit or capital gain to be deferred into years following the year when the sale occurred.

Check with appropriate counsel before using the installment sales method of selling a business.

Tax-Deferred Exchanges - IRC 1031 states, "No gain or loss shall be recognized on the exchange of property held for productive use in a trade or business or for investment if such property is exchanged solely for property of like-kind which is to be held either for productive use in a trade or business or for investment."

Like Kind - When properties exchanged are considered to be like kind, held for productive use in a trade, business or for an investment, no gain is recognized.

Treasury Regulations state that the words "like-kind" refer to the nature or character of the property and not to grade or quality. Like-kind exchanges in real estate may occur between apartments, industrial buildings, commercial land for development or farmland for use in a business.

Three-Party Exchanges - Many times an investor will not want to sell a property because the cost of capital gains taxes are unacceptable. A tax-deferred exchange can be a good strategy to use if a second party with a like-kind property can be found. The two exchange investment properties. If not, a third party may become involved.

In a three-party exchange, a third party agrees to buy a property available only through a tax-deferred exchange. The title of the property available for exchange passes to the new buyer. A qualified intermediary holds money received in the exchange. The seller locates an investment property for sale that would have qualified as a like-kind exchange with the original property sold. The intermediary purchases the property and delivers title to the original selling party. A non-simultaneous, tax-deferred exchange has occurred.

Non-Simultaneous Exchanges - The Tax Reform Act of 1984 provides that a non-simultaneous exchange is a like-kind exchange if it adheres to the following rules. The buyer must identify the property to be acquired within 45 days from the transfer date of the property sold. The buyer must take ownership within the lesser of 180 days from the transfer date of the property sold or the date a tax return is filed for the year in which the transfer of the original property occurred.

Boot - Cash or non-like-kind property received in excess of the fair market value of property relinquished in a tax-deferred exchange is called "boot." Boot is created when the values of the properties exchanged are not equal, which is often the case. To the extent that boot is received, a gain is recognized.

Related Party Exchanges - Sometimes tax benefits are created when related parties exchange properties. One such benefit occurs when the larger gain on one property is shifted onto another with a lower applicable tax rate. If either party sells or disposes of the property received within two years of the exchange date, the original exchange will not be treated as like kind.

Business Expenses and Deductions

Nature of Business Expenses - The IRC discusses what types of expenses may be deductible for business purposes. Generally, acceptable business expenses are those that support profit-motivated activity. They may be deducted from business income, provided they are well documented, not unreasonable, consistent with the business activity, and necessary to insure continued business operations.

Amortization – Intangibles - Businesses are allowed to deduct an expense called amortization. This is the write-off of intangible assets, which is comparable to depreciation or cost recovery for tangible property. Intangible assets are written-off over a wide variety of terms, but always on a straight-line basis. The IRC guidelines pertain to the amortization deductions that may be taken for intangibles purchased including goodwill; start up and organizational expenses are also covered under IRC guidelines.

Types of intangibles include goodwill, covenants not to compete, franchises, trademarks, trade names, licenses, permits or granted rights such as a broadcast license, copyrights, patents, secret formulas or production methods, and competitive intelligence. These assets are deemed to add value to a business.

Depreciation - The IRC refers to depreciation, amortization and cost recovery. These are the periodic write-off, or deduction, of an asset used in a business or investment, which is held for the production of income. The term of depreciation that applies to various types of assets can vary widely.

The depreciation recovery period for real property that was placed in service after 1986 is 27.5 years for residential rental property and 39 years for non-residential real property. Tangible personal property is divided into classes. These are 3-year, 5-year, 7-year, 10-year, 15-year and 20 year.

Two basic methods are used to calculate the amount of depreciation taken. Generally, the method of depreciation taken is determined by the year the property was placed in service. Rules regarding depreciation schedules have changed. After 1986 an accelerated method may be used for personal tangible property but may be converted to the straight-line method when it yields a larger amount. A straight-line method divides the amount that can be depreciated by the number of years in the applicable depreciation period to determine annual depreciation deductions.

Entertainment/Meals - Deductibility of entertainment and meals expenses are covered by IRC regulations. Taking a client to the baseball game or dinner in a five star restaurant is impressive for one while enjoyable for the other. Enforcement problems have developed. IRC regulations disallow certain entertainment expenses, and provide rules that classify, restrict and set standards for record keeping. The reason for clarification is that while business entertainment can be an important business practice the benefit may also inure to the taxpayer.

In addition, any expense for entertainment or meals is subject to a percentage of disallowance. The deduction available is the actual cost of entertainment and meals including beverages and tips and taxes when reduced by one half. This is the amount that can be deducted for qualifying business entertainment and meal expenses.

Home Office Expenses - In 1997 the Taxpayer Relief Act made it possible for home-based entrepreneurs and telecommuters to deduct more expenses related to performing their work from offices in their homes.

A person working at home uses a portion of it for the purposes of producing business income. This qualifies the business owner to receive a deduction on the assets (or portion of assets) that are used in the home. It can be difficult, however, to determine the amount of deduction that may be taken.

To qualify as business-related expenses from the home, one of the following conditions must be present. The home office is used by the taxpayer for any of their trade, professional or business activities, is a meeting location for clients, patients or customers or, the home office used is not attached to the home itself. Employers must also prove the home office is for the benefit of the taxpayer or employer.

Expenses deducted will include those directly related to the office and those that are indirectly related. Direct expenses are decorating costs. Indirect expenses are those that are inherent in the cost of the property and would be calculated as a prorated share of the total. Property taxes, insurance, interest, utilities, repairs, etc., are examples.

Interest - Interest is the cost businesses pay for the use of money. This includes loan points and fees, finance charges and premiums. Interest has been described in this book as part of the cost of financial leverage in a business transaction. Interest incurred on behalf of the business activity, mortgage or otherwise, is deductible in full from business income.

Taxes - Certain types of taxes may be deducted for purposes of calculating federal income taxes. Some examples of taxes that may be deducted are State, local and foreign property taxes paid, and taxes paid in the operation of a business or trade for purposes of producing income. Certain types of personal property taxes are deductible as well.

A few examples of taxes that are not deductible include: Federal income taxes, inheritance taxes, gift taxes, import duties, employer social security contributions, state and local sales taxes or state inheritance and gift taxes.

Travel - Travel expenses are costs incurred by a taxpayer that occur while they are "away from home" and working to further the objectives of their business or employment activity. Qualifying travel expenses may be deducted from income. The IRC rules discuss specific rules that can affect the deductibility of travel expenses.

Transportation - Transportation expenses are generally regarded as travel expenses incurred in the normal course of business while the taxpayer is not away from home.

Index

balance sheet, 25-27, 31, 34-35, 59
bankers, 2, 14, 16, 18, 20-21, 64, 73, 75-79, 104, 117-118, 122-123, 130, 133-140, 148, 160, 163, 189, 250-252
basis, 268
  cash, 266
bill of sale, 253
boot, 225, 227, 271
branded power, 93
breach of agreement, 18
brokers, 1-2, 9, 14, 16, 20, 40, 177, 181-183, 259
bulk sales law, 253-254, 256
business:
  momentum, 172
  plan, 169, 173
buying low, 144-157
capital gains, 119, 165, 221-222, 225-227, 229, 266, 268-270
capital structure, 10, 14, 90
capitalization method, 6, 30, 48, 101-107, 110, 113-114, 150, 208, 211, 237
capitalization (CAP) rates, 70-74, 80-81, 101-107, 151-152, 175, 208-209, 211
cash flow, 4, 10, 37, 39-40, 42, 44, 47-49, 51-55, 59-61, 63-64, 66-67, 69-70, 74-76, 80, 84, 91, 103-104, 106-107, 115-119, 148-149, 151, 154-156, 171-172, 174-175, 179, 187, 207-210, 216, 232-233, 235-236, 245, 258
  free, 48, 66-67, 75-77, 84, 103-104, 106, 109, 111-114, 117, 120-121, 123-126, 137-139, 151-153, 155-156, 174-175, 209-210, 212, 237
  leveraged, *see leveraged cash flow method*
  weighted, 48, 52
cash reserves, 56
central tendency, 6
certificates of good standing, 169, 256, 259

Notes

DATE DUE

Demco